ANATOMY
OF THE
CHOPPER

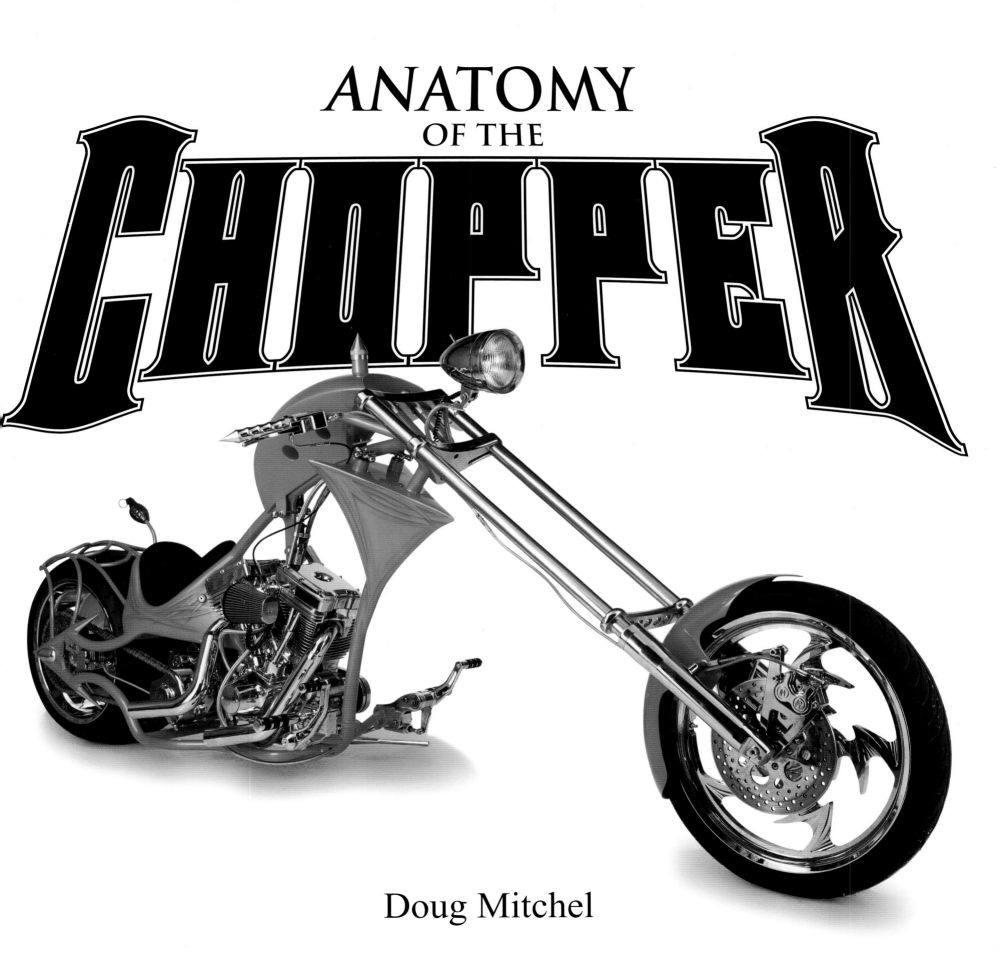

Doug Mitchel

Published by

krause publications
An Imprint of F+W Publications

700 East State Street • Iola, WI 54990-0001
715-445-2214 • 888-457-2873

Our toll-free number to place an order or obtain
a free catalog is (800) 258-0929.

Library of Congress Catalog Number: 2005931489

ISBN 13-digit: 978-0-89689-266-8
ISBN 10-digit: 0-89689-266-2

Designed by Paul Birling
Edited by Brian Earnest

Printed in China

DEDICATION

For my mom, with all my love.

A woman who has survived countless challenges,
the biggest of which was raising the likes of me.

SPECIAL THANKS

To Pain Eriksson, for allowing me to move in and take over his shop so I could photograph choppers during Bike Week in Daytona Beach, Fla. Not only did he sacrifice his working shop for an entire week, but he steered some amazing machines into the lights for this book.

To Dave Harvey and Kathy Schroer of the Heritage Motorcycle Rally for also providing me a great working space to shoot choppers during their second annual Bike Build-Off in Charleston, S.C.

To the crew at Windwalkers Motorcycles of Naperville, Ill., for yet again delivering one of their custom factory machines to be photographed.

To Kevin May for letting me commandeer his spectacular studio to shoot one of the exotic choppers we see in this book.

As always, thanks to the rest of the owners and builders who allowed me to take time out of their busy lives and vacations so I could photograph the machines you see on these pages.

ANATOMY OF THE CHOPPER

CONTENTS

INTRODUCTION

By now, I am fairly certain that you've purchased, or at least have flipped through, the pages of another book spotlighting the world of choppers. The trend is undeniably strong and seems to have no end in sight. New builders show up every day, and exposure on television and other forms of media is increasing.

There seems to be no limits to the imaginations and talents of today's builders as the machines they create stretch the boundaries of art and metal.

With this book, we hope to illustrate what goes into designing and building a modern chopper. Just for comparison, a few old-school models are included to show us where we came from in the universe of building custom motorcycles.

For those whose interest goes beyond looking at the pictures and reading the text, we have also provided a list of builders who showcase their talents and components in these pages. Anyone wanting to build one of their own custom bikes now has an easy reference guide to get them started.

HARLEY-DAVIDSON XL

John Flanigan

The early days of chopper building were much different from today. There wasn't a variety of parts catalogs from which to shop or the vast array of technology we now have at our fingertips. A typical project began with a street-legal machine that was growing weary from everyday use or had even been involved in an accident. The owner could choose to return his bike to its original trim or take it in another direction.

The 1,000-cc motor from Harley-Davidson is mostly stock but has been treated to several appearance upgrades.

This example was one man's dream that ended up in boxes – unfinished and without hope of being completed. The current owner resurrected this basket case and assembled the parts into a worthy chopper. This wasn't done in the old-school style to be different; it really is a machine from the early days, and that alone sets it apart from modern iterations that mimic early machines.

Although purchased in boxes, it was still a Harley-Davidson at its core. The 1,000-cc XL Sportster still had miles of work to be done before it would be usable, but it was a competent base model. The bulk of the motor and its cases remain stock, although copious quantities of chrome and polish were applied to the vintage mill. In the builder's effort to create the look of a Knucklehead motor, the cylinder heads and rocker boxes were reshaped and now are more contoured than the stock shapes. A few upgrades to the motor included higher-compression pistons and an E-model carburetor from S&S. The air cleaner is also from the S&S catalog, and Crane is responsible for the ignition. Keeping the lubricants within operating temperature is an oil cooler from Lockhart. It makes for more confident riding when stuck in traffic. A set of chrome drag pipes point

Gold-plated springs provide some flash and suspension to the front end of the rigid chassis.

A simple drum on the rear wheel is the chopper's only method of braking.

A small peanut tank resides atop the frame rail and carries less than 3 gallons of fuel.

the exhaled fumes in the right direction. A few touches of gold hardware
also can be found on the modified V-twin. The standard four-speed gearbox remains on duty, and a chain provides the final drive.

This example was built with a rigid frame typical of many early and
current choppers. This modification removes any factory suspension from
the cycle's rear end and allows for a clean appearance without the clutter
of shock absorbers. Of course, the ride suffers a bit, but many riders accept
that as part of the experience. In addition to removing the rear suspension,
a rake of 38 degrees was applied to the steering head. To this angle, a girder
front fork measures 6 inches over, giving the bike that popular long, tall
look. The fork's lower legs also were twisted for an added bit of sparkle.
Offsetting the yards of chrome on the forks are gold-plated springs, which
make a nice contrast.

Continental rubber rolls at either end, wrapped around a set of ultra-
classic Invader wheels. These all-steel rims were the way to go when this
chopper was built and still look great today. The square-section spokes are
massive and number five on the front hoop and 10 on the rear. The front
wheel measures 16 inches in diameter; the aft wheel is 19 inches. Braking
was not highly regarded in the old days, so the only evidence of it here is
the minimal drum brake on the rear wheel.

Perhaps the most important aspect of this build is the sheet metal.
Choices of fuel tanks and fenders were fairly limited in the early days,
at least when it came to off-the-shelf items. Builders handy with sheet
metal and a torch could always bend their own, but even that technology was limited compared with today's options. A peanut fuel tank from
S.I.E. was mounted to the upper frame tube and shows how things used to
be done. A ducktail rear fender also harkens back to the roots of chopper
building. Hiding within the rear opening of the fender is an Arlen Ness
cat's-eye taillight. The blue-dot mounted to the lens may not be legal
in many states but looks right at home on this old-world machine. The
chrome oil bag is another bit from S.I.E. and melds perfectly with the XL's
theme. The elongated Predator saddle from Drag Specialties is a modern
piece and looks right at home on this vintage chopper.

Finishing off the job are multiple coats of bronze mixed with gold metallic paint. No early chopper was worth its salt unless treated to some
sort of metal-flake hue, and this example is not about to cause trouble by
bucking that system.

Too many years were taken to reassemble this throwback to the primitive
days of choppers, but the result is well worth the time. Not only does it look
great, it gives some perspective on how they did it in the old days.

AMERICAN IRONHORSE TEXAS CHOPPER

Windwalkers Motorcycles of Naperville

Many custom-chopper buyers turn to a local shop to order and wait for a machine built to their specifications. This process yields any number of variations, but the expense and time required may exceed some buyers' guidelines. Also, many hand-built choppers open the door to possible troubles because of the mixing and matching of their components. This is not to say that high-end custom rides are not dependable, but for some buyers, a "factory" chopper, complete with dealer network and warranty, is the only way to go.

Your choice of 111-, 117- or 124-cubic-inch motors can be installed in your AIH Texas Chopper.

There have been many factory offerings in chopper history, but only a few remain today. Of the surviving brands, American IronHorse of Fort Worth, Texas, offers buyers a choice of six models. Also, each machine is built to satisfy the specific tastes of the person writing the check. A factory bike from American IronHorse is a safer alternative to a hand-built custom.

Before you state your case for not wanting to be seen on the same factory bike as your neighbor's, the American IronHorse program allows a vast array of options and accessories that deliver a highly customized machine, even in its factory-based form.

After the buyer selects one of AIH's six models, the customizing process begins. The example shown here is the Texas Chopper, and as with all AIH models, it provides a great platform on which to order your own copy. The Texas Chopper includes a long list of factory trim, making it a great place to begin your design. Thirty-eight degrees of frame rake provide the long, lean look, and the front forks also are stretched 12 inches, adding to the Texas Chopper's stance. A set of polished triple trees add another 4 degrees of angle to the steering equation, and the handlebars are chrome for looks and endurance. At the top of the polished trees you find a digital AIH dashboard, which keeps the rider up to date on the vital signs.

A 12-over front fork reaches out and is polished to a mirror finish.

Lighting the way is a massive 5 3/4-inch headlight, making nighttime riding a snap.

A digital instrument housing lives atop the polished triple trees and is readable in any lighting condition.

The elongated fuel tank adds more visual length to the already extended Texas Chopper.

Of the many polished components found on the Texas Chopper, the transfer case and six-speed transmission cover are some of the most prominent.

The headlight measures nearly 6 inches in diameter, providing ample wattage for nighttime cruising. The fork legs' lower sections are glassy smooth and polished within an inch of their life. Buffed components are found all over the Texas Chopper, as evidenced by the forward controls, side-mount license plate, four-piston front brake calipers, and right-side drive transmission cover. The case contains six forward gears of close-ratio design. The right-side configuration provides added stability under hard acceleration and a better balanced machine.

Between the front fork legs are a 21-inch wheel and tire package ensconced by an AIH chopper fender. Speaking of wheels, the AIH catalog offers 10 designs. Who says "factory" has to be dull? With wheel names like "Rattler," "Trouble" and "Dragula," you can be assured of some excitement in the hoop department. Regardless of the style, each rim is highly polished for your viewing pleasure.

Topping off the large-diameter tube frame is a super-stretched fuel tank that leads all the way to the saddle's leading edge. An internally supported rear fender partially covers the massive 280-millimeter rear tire, and a stealth swing arm holds the wheel and tire in place.

Once you've chosen the bike, a suitable power plant must be added. The standard V-twin measures 111 cubic inches and delivers a potent

The truncated rear fender hides just enough of the massive 280-millimeter tire that lies beneath.

punch while carrying a two-year warranty. Upgrading to the 117-cubic-inch mill delivers more bang, but the warranty is trimmed to one year. An even larger 124-cubic-inch monster can be installed if you feel the need for real speed. Since buyers of the 124 are probably not seeking a faster way to their house of worship on Sundays, their aggressive riding style is addressed by a six-month warranty. Staggered gooseneck drag pipes and a retro air cleaner can be checked off on the accessory list for any of the three motors.

Next, the buyer selects a custom color set and graphics for his mount. Base models come with a choice of solid colors sans graphics, and in addition, a range of 18 base colors can be combined with any of the 33 graphics options shown on the Web site. This dizzying array of hues and artwork guarantees the exclusivity of your AIH machine. Once colors have been chosen, another list of accessories can be added to bring your chopper to the next level of custom. Many of these items can be added or altered later as your tastes become more focused.

Seven different saddles, eight variations of sissy bars, and a four-pack of rear-view mirrors await buyers. Special grips and enhanced rider and passenger foot pegs also are included in the catalog. In keeping with the tuner-car trend, L.E.D. turn signals covered by clear lenses also can be installed on any AIH chopper.

BRITT MOTORSPORTS

The world is full of choices, even in the chopper arena. Most products built today are powered by a Harley-Davidson V-twin or clone motors of varying displacements, but some prefer something different between their tubes. Having the same train of thought, Scott Britt put his years of experience with Yamaha into chopper production. Two Britt Motorsports creations are shown here, but the company's Web site and catalog offer many more choices.

In his younger days, Scott toiled in his father's Yamaha dealership, exposing him to the terrific line of models produced by the Asian manufacturer. Today, nearly three decades later, Scott is still up to his ears in the Yamaha brand, focusing on custom-built metric choppers. Metric choppers are not new; Honda's inline-4 CB750 was often the donor for frame and motor as individuals spun out creations of their own desire. The 1970s were hardly the high-tech world we know today, so some of the machines lacked, shall we say, finesse. The early chopper phase waned but never disappeared, leaving the door open for fresh ideas and greater use of modern technology.

Britt Motorsports machines have graced the covers of many magazines in recent years, proving their viability in a universe filled with American-powered machines. Each machine shown here fits a different category, but each is done with precision and a high level of craftsmanship. Not only are these choppers amazing to look at and ride, but their prices make them even more attractive to those who want a chopper but don't feel the need for a Milwaukee vibrator in the frame. For those who might think metric is only a passing fad, a new television show covering the expanding world of metric customs was scheduled for release in 2006. We'll be sure to see a Britt bike before too long.

YAMAHA ROADSTER

Britt Motorsports

cott Britt considers this cycle his first true original. Starting with a clean slate, Scott designed the frame with a 42-degree rake and a stretch of 4 inches. His choppers have more contemporary power plants, but he retained the old-school rigid layout for the rear end. The pro-street chassis was penned to carry a 300-series tire and wheel out back. Steering the bike is a set of Britt custom forks that are also 2 inches over. Holding the fork tubes in place is a set of Britt custom triple trees, anodized to match the sheet metal's blue paint. The bars also are Britt custom components and are finished off with grips from

The factory Yamaha Roadster motor was bumped to 108 cubic inches to deliver more motivation to the 300-millimeter rear tire.

A fuel tank from Thunderbike holds the precious commodity in style and is trimmed with a classic flame paint job.

Arlen Ness. Brake and clutch levers are alloy billet and hail from Performance Machine. The wheels are spoked models from DNA and bring a touch of classic to this modern cycle. A 21-inch hoop up front is teamed with the 300-millimeter-wide by 18-inch loop under the rear fender. Avon Venom rubber keeps both rims safe from the abrasive pavement.

Slowing the beast is a hodgepodge of hardware designed to provide the proper amount of braking. The front brake rotor is a drilled unit from Kustomwerks and is grabbed by a Yamaha factory caliper. Performance

Machine is responsible for the front master cylinder. The drive sprocket and rear brake rotor are combined in a single unit called a "sprotor" from K-Tech. The rear caliper is also from K-Tech.

Not wanting to reinvent the entire machine from scratch, Scott placed a Freestyle fuel tank from Thunderbike atop the upper frame tube. It gracefully arches back to reach the saddle. The oil bag is Yamaha, but the flat cover also is from Thunderbike. A front fender from Milwaukee Iron was modified for this bike; the rear shield hails from Kustomwerks and

A pair of Weber carburetors dole out the fuel and air mixture with precision.

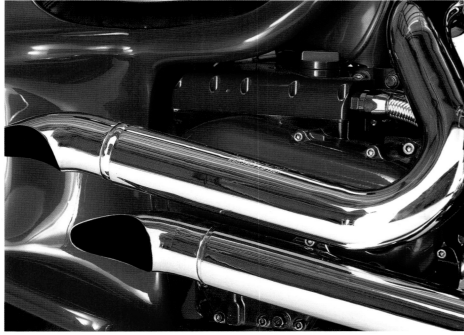
A set of large-diameter exhaust pipes, bent by Britt Motorsports for this machine, provide a quick exit for spent gases.

The forks, triple trees and handlebars are all hand formed by Britt Motorsports, making a unique statement.

Both sides of the motor are treated to a large dose of anodized components that match the bike's Tru-Blue Pearl paint to a "T".

Having the propulsion and braking components on the right side leaves the DNA spoke wheel open for viewing.

also was reconfigured to fit the Britt custom. With a width of 13 inches, the curved metal can barely contain the 10 1/2-inch-wide tire under it. While you're pounding the road with the massive rear tire, a set of pegs and forward controls from Supreme Legends give your boots a place to roost. The saddle is yet another custom piece from Britt's mind and sits low in the drop-seat rigid frame.

All of this rolling artwork would mean nothing without power, and the Yamaha mill was beefed up to provide plenty of that. Displacing 108 cubic inches, the motor features a pair of Patrick slugs sliding in the Yamaha jugs. The balance of the motor's internals are stock Yamaha, a testament to the design's strength. A pair of

Weber carbs mixes the air and fuel before sending them into the cylinders, and a Dyna 3000 ignition provides the energy for the plugs to light the mixture into action. Spent fumes are sent packing through a set of Britt-bent tubes with no mention of noise reduction. The factory Yamaha five-speed gearbox sends the power to the rear wheel with the help of a Barnett clutch and chain drive that replaces the factory propulsion system.

A basic yet beautiful Tru-Blue Pearl paint from House of Kolor was applied to the Roadster with a large quantity of bits treated to a matching anodized blue. The classic flames begin at the head of the fuel tank and lick their way back to the dropped saddle. Six weeks were required to put the package together.

BRITT BUD BIKE

Britt Motorsports

In contrast to the long, lean and low Roadster, this bike follows a more traditional chopper avenue yet still carries a Yamaha motor in its frame. The apparent NASCAR theme was not Scott Britt's original intention, but as the red and black paint was viewed, it simply came to pass. The "Bud" in the title actually refers to the rider's name, thus avoiding any legal activity, or at least they hope.

A Prince Tech chassis was the starting point but was modified by Britt Motorsports. A 4-inch stretch was applied to the upper tube along with a 42-degree rake. Front forks

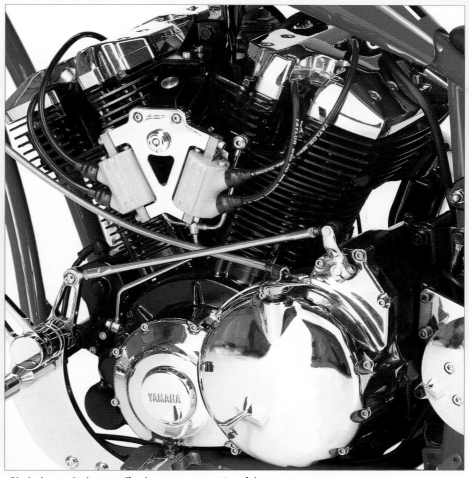

Blacked-out cylinders are offset by a generous portion of chrome components.

again are Britt products and measure 43 millimeters in diameter. The 8-inch addition to the length throws the handlebars high in the air in true chopper style. The triple trees are more Britt components and hold a set of Yamaha bars in place. Control levers also are straight from the Yamaha parts bin. Forward controls are Legends brand and place the rider in a stretched-out posture that's all the rage. Built as a more traditional chopper, the bike has no rear suspension. Sheet metal hails from all corners of the States. Britt stretched the Wyatt Gatlin tank to fit the motif. A Thunderbike oil bag holds the lubricant in place. Front fender is by Milwaukee Iron, the rear by Kustomwerks.

As with every bike Britt Motorsports builds, any part purchased from an outside source is modified before use. A set of Slash wheels from RC Components graces both ends of the machine – 2 1/2 inches by 21 inches between the forks and 8 1/2 inches by 18 inches at the business end. Black powder coating sets the stage for the NASCAR theme and offsets

Front binders also hail from Yamaha on this Britt custom.

◄ A factory Yamaha mill powers the Bud Bike and displaces 1600 cc's.

the chrome mill and Kosmic Red bodywork quite nicely. The fiery hue is another House of Kolor flavor. Avon Venom rubber makes for a smoother ride than the rims alone can muster. A fairly moderate 250-series rear tire is mounted to the back rim but still provides plenty of traction for everyday use, unless your everyday use includes runs at the local drag strip. Factory Yamaha components provide the braking power at both wheels.

Keeping with the traditional chopper layout, the Bud Bike rolls with a standard-displacement Roadster motor. The 1600 cc's are nothing to sneeze at, and Britt installed some additional toys to accent the Yamaha V-twin. A pair of Patrick pistons resides within the cylinder walls, and a Mikuni 42-millimeter carburetor, complete with flat slides, monitors the explosive mix heading into the motor. An air cleaner from Baron's cleans the air before it enters the combustion chambers. Electricity for the plugs is delivered via a Dyna 3000 ignition system. Yamaha provides the five-speed gearbox and final drive.

This machine has captured the attention of many publishers, despite the speedy three-week build time. Its appearance on two magazine covers and an Iron Angle calendar proves the chopper-buying audience is beginning to accept machines powered by import mills.

SPEEDWAY CHOPPERS

Randy Reeves has an extensive background in top-fuel drag racing and decided to turn to the chopper world to see what he could accomplish there. With four years of bike building behind him, Randy joined forces with Frank Weiss Racing Components. The company offered nearly three decades of experience producing racing components that met the highest standards. Now, with a complete machine shop and engineering department at Randy's disposal, his Speedway Choppers could turn up the heat in the competitive world of high-end customs.

Randy Reeves

SPEEDWAY CHOPPERS LS1

Speedway Choppers

aving an engineering and machine shop as part of his new-found chopper-building efforts allowed Randy to design and build some radical and unique machines. The LS1's chassis is a Speedway Choppers original, including the rear swing arm. Only a fully stocked C&C department is capable of cranking out this level of component, and its efforts are featured on this super-clean chopper. The

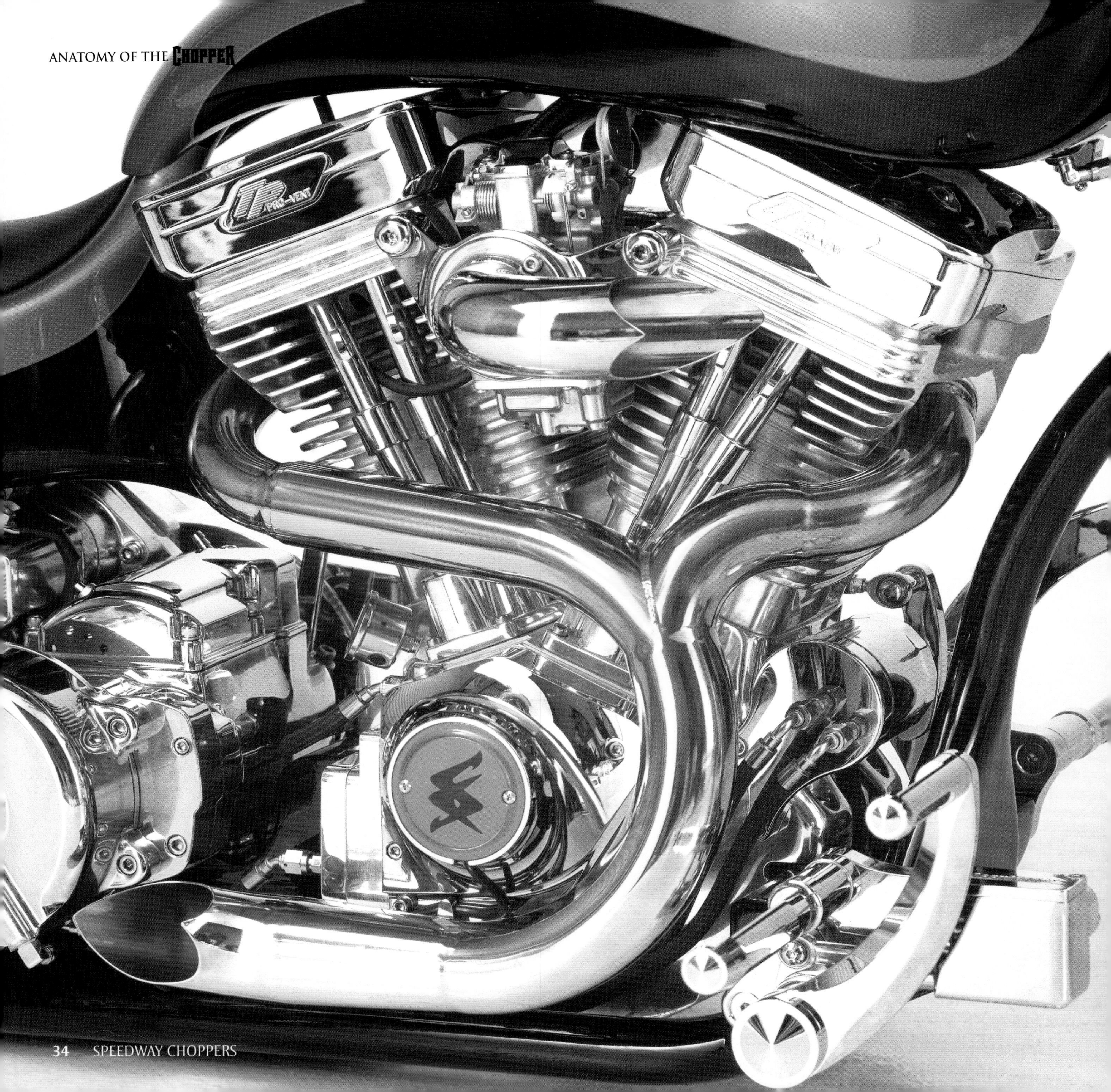
PRO-VENT

frame's design incorporates a built-in oil tank and rigid rear fender that moves with the chassis when the air suspension is activated. The Smart Air system is the brainchild of the Air Lift Co. and automatically adjusts the ride height to acommodate the rider's weight. When parking the LS1, you might search for the flip-out kickstand found on most motorcycles. Kickstand? We don't need no stinking kickstand. Just hit the button and drop the LS1 frame rails to the ground. There's easy mount and dismount courtesy of the super-low saddle height. Then again, the 300-millimeter

rear tire is almost enough to balance the bike, but the Smart Air system still adds a big bunch of cool.

A 43-degree rake also adds the right mix of steering angle to make the LS1 handle as good as it looks. A Perse Performance spherical front fork continues the sleek contours of the LS1. Perse 5-degree triple trees hold everything in place along with the Speedway Chopper Stainless Steel Drags handlebars. Perse handgrips are mated to Performance Machine control levers. Foot pegs and controls are part of the Accutronics line of billet componentry.

The Sputhe primary carries power from the motor to the transmission in style.

◀ A 116-cubic-inch Total Performance motor keeps the LS1 in motion. The Speedway Choppers exhaust does the same for the exiting gases.

A Weld Racing 65-tooth drive pulley is found at the business end of the drive belt.

The Weld Racing Slash front wheel matches the rear hoop, drive pulley and front rotor.

The Fat Katz fuel tank was stretched 4 inches to meet the long, sleek lines of the LS1.

The most obvious element of the LS1's design is the flowing bodywork. Fat Katz was the choice for the fuel tank and front and rear fenders, and all were altered for the LS1. The 535 aluminum tank was stretched 4 inches to add to the contoured lines. The closed tunnel keeps things clean from every angle. The front fender is a Yuma, and the rear rubber shield is a Houston F150 – an appropriate name considering how much real estate it has to cover. The rear fender also was modified to mount rigidly to the swing arm so it could move when the suspension was activated. An L.E.D. strip was melded into the rear setup to provide a bright taillight when the brakes are applied. The Speedway Choppers oil tank stretches back into the frame to appear as

a single, seamless unit. Punctuating the gleaming Cinnamon and Pitch Black paint is a saddle covered in black vinyl by Stitches. The seat itself is another Speedway Choppers original.

When you're riding the LS1, Weld Racing Slash wheels keep things rolling smoothly. Leading the pack is an 18-inch by 3 1/2-inch rim covered in Metzeler ME880 rubber. Bringing up the rear is an 18-inch by 10 1/2-inch monster wrapped with an Avon Venom tire. Weld Racing is also responsible for the matching Slash front brake rotor and rear 65-tooth drive pulley. An HHI Soft Tail caliper grabs the front rotor; the rear braking is all Speedway Choppers parts. This ensemble was created from an 8-inch disc halted by a two-piston caliper.

Perse front forks and triple trees are mated to an Accutronics headlight and Dakota digital gauge cluster.

All of this beauty and technology would be wasted without a motor, and Total Performance was called to fill the void. Displacing 116 cubic inches, the TP motor features cams with a 0.650 lift for smooth delivery of the ponies within. Feeding the twin-cylinder mill is a Mikuni 45-millimeter carburetor fitted with a Speedway Choppers stainless-steel velocity stack. TP single-fire ignition provides the spark, and a Speedway Choppers RSFSP stainless-steel exhaust rapidly expels the fumes away

from the motor. The two-into-one design is truncated by a spade-shaped opening at the end, adding another terrific detail to the creation. Six speeds are available through the Accessories Unlimited right-side drive gearbox. A Sputhe clutch assembly and primary transfer power from the motor to the transmission effortlessly.

Only three weeks were required to build the LS1, a true testament to the powers of the R&D and C&C gods.

BRYANT 1

Speedway Choppers

With the success of its previous builds growing rapidly, Speedway Choppers was approached by the Bryant heating and cooling systems company to build a corporate theme bike. It wasn't a market Speedway planned to enter, but it allowed the company to show its prowess in building to a customer's demands. One of Bryant's demands was that the bike be ready for a trade show only four weeks away. This time crunch put the Speedway team in high gear.

To begin, Speedway selected its own B1 frame and then added its single-sided 240 swing arm. The Air Lift Co. again provided the Smart Air suspension for the tail, allowing the rider to adjust the ride height. The frame's geometry included a rake of 40 degrees with 6 inches out and 2 inches up. Low and long was the name of the game when drawing up the Bryant 1. A Fat Katz rear fender was molded into the frame for a seamless, flowing appearance. American Suspension was tapped for its inverted front forks, which were stretched 4 inches. Six-degree triple trees again from American Suspension made a nice home for the Speedway Choppers' radius stainless-steel handlebars. Mounted to the upper triple tree is one of the Bryant 1's slickest bits: The instrument cluster was built from scratch and looks just like a home thermostat. The digital readout appears in a small window encased in a billet housing. The devil is in the details, and Speedway knows how to nail them down.

A 120-cubic-inch motor from Ultima adds plenty of go to this otherwise show bike.

Although built mostly as a show bike, the Bryant 1 has plenty of go in it. An Ultima 120-cubic-inch V-twin lives between the frame tubes, delivering more punch than a show bike deserves. The polished motor breathes in through an S&S Super G carb outfitted with a Speedway Choppers velocity stack that was altered to mimic a Bryant heat exchanger. Details, details. A Dyna 2000I ignition delivers the spark, and an RSLFP exhaust from Speedway hastens the exit of departing fumes. Power from the Ultima motor

transfers through a Sputhe primary to the Accessories Unlimited six-speed, right-side drive tranny.

A clutch from Sputhe allows for smooth shifts no matter the rpm. Weld Racing provided the 65-tooth rear pulley.

Sheet-metal sources were varied. An Independence fuel tank was purchased and stretched 5 inches. Speedway crafted its own oil bag and then blended it into the frame's contours. Fat Katz fenders were chosen

The all-polished mill adds to the sanitary nature of the bike's composition.

The tire-hugging front fender also received its own louvers.

The innovative Speedway Choppers team turned out this amazing instrument cluster, which looks like a home thermostat.

for both tires; modifications ensured a unique appearance. Louvers on the trailing edges of both fenders were a Speedway touch, adding a subtle detail to the chopper's otherwise loud expression. Hand and foot controls are from the Accutronics catalog and are joined by control levers from Performance Machine.

Pro-1 mirrors let the rider see with clarity who was just passed. The taillight and license plate holder are Speedway Choppers originals, and the tag frame was molded into the rear fender for slickness and style. The solo saddle is simple and tastefully wrapped in smooth, black vinyl for comfort and cleanliness.

Keeping the chassis off the ground is a set of Weld Racing Chopper wheels. The aft hoop measures 18 inches by 8 1/2 inches; the front rim sits at 18 inches by 3 1/2 inches. Metzeler ME880 rubber keeps it all off the road. A Weld Racing Chopper front rotor is hugged by a caliper from HHI; the rear slowing power is all Speedway Choppers gear. An 8-inch stainless-steel rotor is snagged by a two-piston caliper, and Speedway's patented trans brake aids deceleration.

VOODOO CHOPPERS

Eric Gorges didn't start out wanting to build custom choppers, but always liked working with his hands and creating things of his own design. His first build was an ironhead Sportster, which was the impetus for going beyond that simple project. While working a full-time job, Eric fell seriously ill. After recovering, he decided not to waste his life doing anything less than what he wanted to do. His interests in building motorcycles never disappeared, so he opened his first commercial venture in April 1999.

His first shop was a 500-square-foot garage that was part of his living quarters. Before jumping too deeply into building high-caliber machines, he studied under several metal-working masters. These men taught him how to shape metal to meet customers' needs and to never settle for anything less than perfection. Those skills and traits were brought to his own shop and still exist today as he turns out some of the wildest two-wheeled pieces of sculpture on the road. As his abilities grew, so did his client list. He soon moved his fledgling business into bigger quarters. The new work space was 2,500 square feet and packed with every type of metal-forming and machining equipment available. He made the move in September 2001, and no one on the team has looked back since.

Still working mostly by hand, Eric and his crew take a customer's ideas and turn out something that exceeds even their wildest expectations. Eric's desire never to settle for second best has landed Voodoo Choppers' machines in several major publications and earned a slot on the popular Discovery Channel series *Biker Build-Off*. This program pits two bike builders against each other to see who can design and build the more unusual cycle in only 30 days. After the contest bikes are created and assembled, they are ridden for several hundred miles to an event where final judging is held. The public attending the show can vote for their favorite creation, and the winner goes on to compete against another builder. The prize money and trophy may not be spectacular, but the value of television exposure and winning the build-off boosts the builder's reputation and sometimes his bottom line.

Eric Gorges

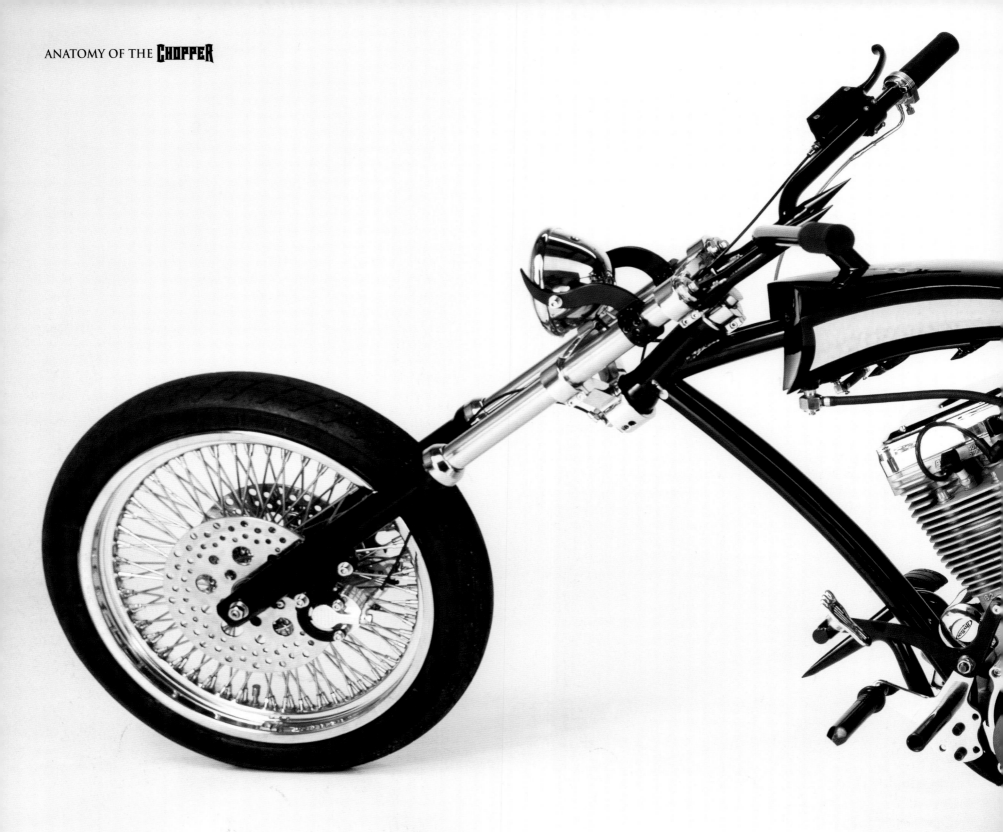

WHISKEY TANGO

Voodoo Choppers

Even a person with little or no chopper-building experience can see that Whiskey Tango is not an off-the-shelf chopper. From the chassis tubes's open layout to the extreme rake of the forks and the wild sheet-metal fuel tank, there is nothing common about this creation. Eric Gorges began building this craft for his own use, but a customer saw it being built and bought it from him. Eric and Voodoo Choppers then completed construction.

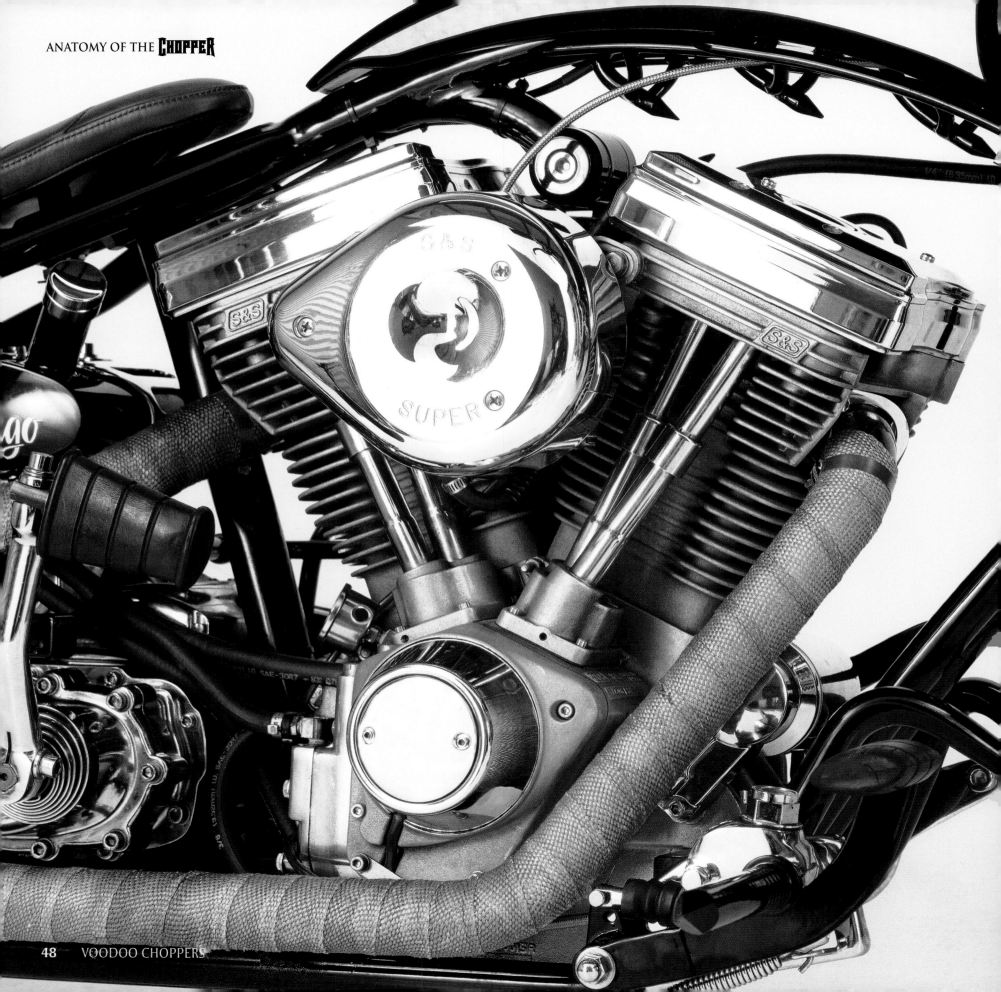

The Digger frame is a Voodoo Choppers design and carries the front forks at a 45-degree rake. No self-respecting chopper builder would even consider adding rear suspension, so the Digger is a hard-tail. A set of Harley-Davidson forks measures 39 millimeters in diameter and was stretched 2 inches, but they do little for the suspension because of their steep angle of rake. Another Voodoo Choppers component is the set of Hot Rod triple-trees that hold the fork tubes in place and provide stability. Because of the geometry, the front tire moves up and down before the fork legs can compress. Who said chopper riding was supposed to be comfortable anyway? Many steel spikes protrude dangerously from Whiskey Tango, adding to the fun in a crash. Talk about body piercing!

The handlebar risers provide another set of lethal points. The actual bars jut wildly from the straight risers. Traditional Harley-Davidson handgrips finish off the black tubes with JayBrake hand controls within the rider's grasp. Being hand-built, this and other Voodoo Choppers machines have few typical angles and assemblies.

The miniscule fuel tank also was fashioned from scratch and holds only 1 gallon. Perhaps the riding position and minimal suspension are in perfect synch with the small fuel capacity. The sharply angled receptacle sweeps back to the rider's pillion and is creased and graceful at the same time, not an easy accomplishment. Residing beneath the Voodoo Choppers solo leather saddle, complete with upholstery by George Paul, is

The simple rear fender shape is complemented by the chrome ladder and wing-nut ensemble.

◄ The S&S V-twin displaces 113 cubic inches and delivers ample power to Whiskey Tango's rear rubber.

another custom piece – the kidney-shaped oil tank. A diagonal filler tube pokes out from the top of the multiple-curved surface and provides easy access when adding a quart of lubrication.

The rear fender, also hand-fabbed, is an odd combination of smooth black steel mated to a chrome ladder, complete with matching chrome wing nuts. Avoiding the trap of more contemporary alloy or billet wheels, Whiskey Tango rolls on spoke rims by American Wire Wheel. A 19-inch front hoop carries 80 glittering spokes, and a 16-inch rim carries the rear donut. Avon is responsible for the rubber at both ends. When stopping for gas, CCI brake rotors accomplish the task. A pair of 10-inch discs up front is joined by a single 11 1/2-inch on the rear. JayBrake made the calipers that pressure the rotors, and Fabricator Kevin's Steel Chopper Parts

crafted the custom mounts for the front units. (A Kevin's machine can be seen elsewhere in this book.)

The motor may be the most mundane part of Whiskey Tango. Although any mill coming from S&S can hardly be called dull, even its 113 cubic inches pale compared with the rest of this handcrafted bike. About the only highly polished items on this chopper are the cylinder heads and case covers on the motor.

An S&S G carburetor metes out the proper punishment when the throttle is twisted hard, and a Dyna ignition keeps the spark hot no matter the attempted velocity. A six-speed Baker gearbox sends the selected gears through a clutch and primary by BDL. On a bike such as this, nothing but a suicide shifter is permitted, and Eric made sure to include that feature in the mix. Upon leaving the motor, spent exhaust gases make their way through a set of Voodoo Chopper pipes, both of which include a spark plug inserted into their exit orifices. By loading the engine with an overly rich fuel mixture and hitting the igniter, the spent gases turn into a freak show of flame-throwing fun. The pair of uneven tubes are wrapped from stem to stern with heat tape for aesthetics and more efficient thermal properties. And it looks great, too.

Small details that wrap up Whiskey Tango include the Voodoo Choppers foot controls and pegs and license-plate frame. Even when you're riding a machine that defies definition, the law prefers you carry the proper identification. At least that way it can tell who's riding, even if it can't tell what's being ridden. House of Kolor Black with Gold Leaf tank insets and graphics complete the appearance package.

Slang for "white trash," Whiskey Tango is anything but. It is, however, another rolling showcase of Eric Gorges' talent and creativity.

JAMES DEAN TRIBUTE

Owner: Brian Hatton

T he year 2004 marked the 50th anniversary of the fateful day when James Dean, youthful movie star and all-around talented guy, was killed in an auto accident while driving a Porsche 550 Spyder. To many, he remains an icon of American movie history, but to some, the car is still the star of the story. It's sad to lose any person so young in life, but when a rare and beautiful automobile is involved, it gets us car guys all weepy.

Brian Hatton mounted a full-blown event to remember Dean's death. That effort included building a series of choppers reflecting the 550's styling. The first one completed became part of a James Dean *Rebel on the Road Tour, by Action Performance* that visited a number of U.S. cities. After the event and tour, only a select number of these custom-built cycles were offered for sale. The bikes were assembled in Dean's hometown of Fairmount, Ind.

Built around a drag-style frame from the German firm HPU, the James Dean Tribute bike steers with a rake of 40 degrees, lending to the bike's long and low profile. A 6-inch stretch to the upper frame tube and an-

No, it's not a Porsche engine. It's a 100-cubic-inch RevTech power plant.

other 6 inches added to the geometry dropped the frame rails almost to the ground, although a side stand is still required when parked. The rear swing arm is another HPU item, and it was modified by drilling and sleeving a number of openings into its length. This same metal aeration treatment was used on the 550's accelerator pedal.

The swing arm was teamed up with suspension from Progressive for a smooth, comfortable ride. Mean Street components were applied to the front-end assembly, including the forks and triple trees. Both Slick models, the lower fork legs and both triple trees were black anodized to accent the rear suspension components, which were also treated in the

The fuel tank's muscular haunches flash back to the Porsche 550 Spyder's bulging fenders.

A Harley-Davidson V-Rod sacrificed its headlight for use on the Tribute bike, and it looks right at home.

The rear fender is complete with pumped-up shoulders, radiator vents, and the "Little Bastard" name borrowed from James Dean's Spyder.

same glossy black finish. The ovoid headlight was borrowed from a modern Harley-Davidson V-Rod, bringing a bit of the latest millennium to the machine's vintage look. White Bros. handlebars are finished with Performance Machine Contour brake and clutch levers. Thunderheart foot pegs and shift and braking controls are part of the assembly.

The fuel tank and rear fender carry the Porsche 550 theme further. Both sections of sheet metal were lovingly formed to mimic the muscular shoulders of the 550 it represents.

The fuel tank has an almost flat top, which is flanked by two sensuously curved segments that taper back to the rear of the storage space. An alloy flip-up fuel cap is another styling cue that hails directly from the 550.

The rear fender covers a 300-millimeter Avon Venom R tire, allowing for plenty of real estate to be formed. The fender's gently curved surface also is fitted with a set of sinewy forms that lead back to meet a pair of

taillights that are complete with chrome bezel trim – very Porsche 550. Resting between these shapely forms is a pair of radiator grilles like those found on the 550's rear deck. All of these design components make a convincing statement of a two-wheeled Porsche. Hey, Porsche now builds a sport-ute and soon a sedan. So why not a cycle, too? The front fender also is custom formed but lacks the swooping, supple rises found on the tank and rear fender. Beneath it lies another Avon Venom R hunk of rub-

ber. Seating on the Tribute is limited to one with a custom-made saddle covered in a red vinyl to again harken back to the 550's interior.

One of the Tribute's most apparent links to the Porsche is the set of specially machined wheels. Cut and shaped to resemble the 550's steel wheels, they bring the bike to another level of replica. Measuring 18 inches by 10 1/2 inches on the rear and 21 inches by 3 inches up front, they hold the tires in place and earn their own spot in history. Brak-

The 550 Spyder was the inspiration for the James Dean Tribute bike.

ing hardware is a bit more ordinary, if you can call anything from Exile Cycles ordinary. A single Exile rotor is mounted to the left side of the front rim, and one of Exile's patented sprotor rear-disc and drive-sprocket combination is used on the rear. An HHI caliper slows the front disc's progress, and an Exile caliper squeezes the forward motion from the rear.

Unlike the four-cam motor used in the Porsche, the Tribute has a 100-cubic-inch RevTech V-twin riding in the rails. A 42-millimeter Mikuni carburetor is fitted with a Joker air cleaner and velocity stack. A RevTech ignition still provides the spark. The black exhaust pipes are another custom bit from *Cooper Bros. and Brian Hatton* and they are Jet-Coated for resistance to heat and discoloration. The Barnett clutch slips power from the six-speed RevTech mill through a Harley-Davidson primary. Final drive is a good old-fashioned chain, which wraps around the Exile sprotor.

The silver hue is reminiscent of the 550, and the "Little Bastard" moniker of Dean's Spyder was placed at the trailing edge of the rear fender, another fitting tribute to a fallen star.

◄ A 103-cubic-inch Panhead mill powers Pyro's Woody and makes the perfect statement for this modern vintage scoot.

PYRO'S WOODY

Rich "Pyro" Pollack

When some builders begin to assemble their customs, they have a rough idea of what they want and may go through several changes before reaching the final product. Before Rich "Pyro" Pollack ever set a wrench in motion, he knew what his final creation would look like. It took two years to locate all the required bits and pieces and to assemble them into the bike shown here. His job as a firefighter is perilous but also affords him some free time to work and play. Rich wanted his bike to capture the essence of the classic era as well as more contemporary times, so he set out to find the components that would accomplish his goals. At first glance, the bike seems to be a great balance of old and new, but upon closer examination, you find countless details that really make a statement. Although subtle, each chosen piece adds to the overall allure.

True to a classic chopper, a rigid diamond chassis was chosen as the platform. A 6-inch stretch was added to the top tube, followed by 12 inches to the front frame tubes. The 45-degree rake is fairly radical but looks right at home on Pyro's Woody. A springer front fork from Paughco handles the front suspension. Rich crafted flat drag bars from nine individual segments of steel that were bar milled and fitted with dice in each end. The ball milled grips are also a Rich original. Dice and gambling are the theme on this modern, old-world machine.

The risers are another handmade bit, topped off with discs of bird's-eye maple. Topping off the fork springs are a set of crystal balls. (Insert joke here.) Maintaining a true vintage outlook, the headlight is actually a spotlight borrowed from a 1950s Chrysler product. The taillight was once found in the center of a 1953 Oldsmobile Rocket steering wheel and was highly modified for use on Pyro's Woody. Forward controls were crafted to include the "pecker head" logo of Crane Cams, but the Thrush exhaust mascot also comes to mind. Ball milled rider and passenger foot pegs match the handgrips perfectly.

Additional dice were installed in the ends of the grips.

S&S cases hold the Panhead motor components in their right locations, and the cylinders displace 103 cubic inches. Carburetion comes from an S&S E model with an air cleaner formed from a 1958 Harley-Davidson police siren cover. A Crane Single-Fire ignition sets things in motion, and handmade exhaust pipes lead the exhaled fumes away. Surrounding the ignition key opening is an old-time bottle opener, adding another touch of nostalgia. A hot-water faucet handle controls the fuel flow through the petcock, and a fire-truck choke handle performs the same function here.

The front forks are from Paughco, but the handlebars are more handmade pieces formed from nine sections of tubing.

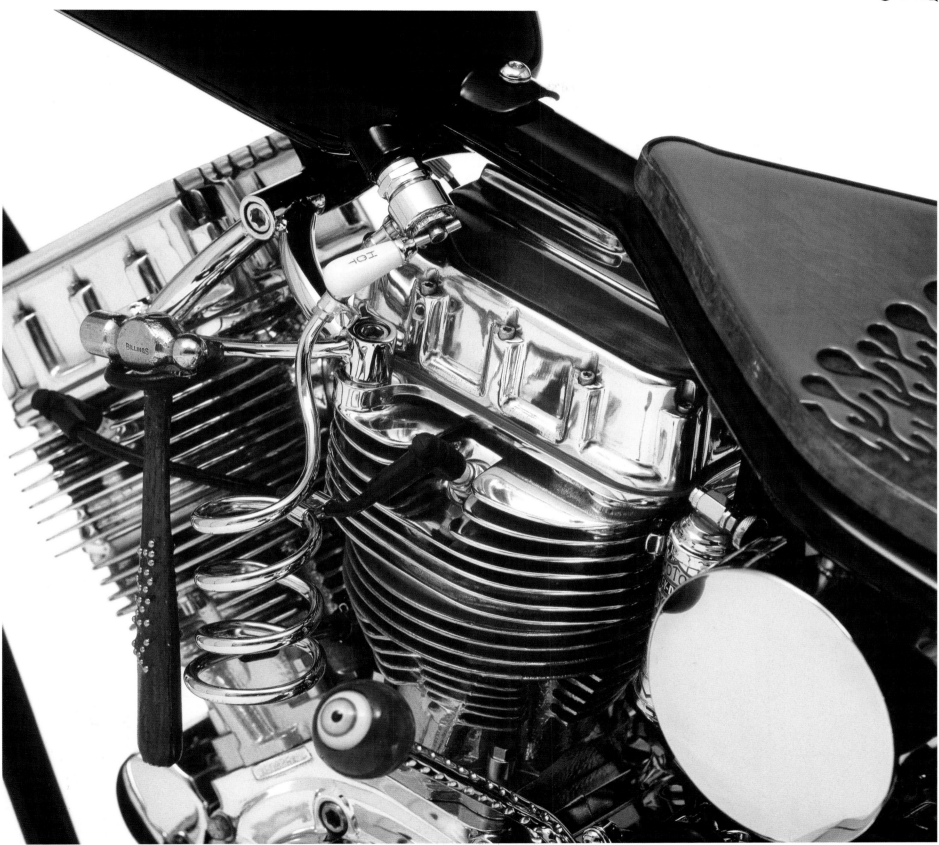

Not the friendliest of details, this hammer is meant to discourage cars from running the chopper off the road.

Inlaid in the side of the primary case is a poker chip from a Las Vegas burlesque house. Nestled by the motor and frame is a vintage Harley fire extinguisher finished in gleaming chrome. The twisted coil of steel tubing feeds the carburetor and adds some fun to the mix.

Each of the curved exits was crafted from four pieces of tubing and then welded, ground and polished to reach their final form. Wrapped with heat-resistant tape, the staccato tubes would look right at home on any drag-racing bike. The brackets holding these items were created from links of chain fused into a solid bracket. Gear selection is made by grabbing the bird's-eye maple and eyeball suicide shift knob mounted suicide style.

This bit of hardware is connected to a RevTech five-speed tranny complete with kick-start pedal. The pedal's typical rubber bits have been exchanged for handmade wooden items. BDL provided the clutch and primary, allowing for everything to shift and transfer smoothly. Both of the flame pulley covers were cut by hand and then polished to blinding beauty. Using aluminum proved to be more difficult than first planned, but the results were worth the effort. Nothing other than spoke wheels would fulfill Rich's dream, so that's what you find at both axles. Three-horned knock-offs adorn both wheels as well, complete with their own dice set into the tips. As with most of the metal components on this chopper, Rich made the knockoffs from scratch. Front braking power is derived from a Russell rotor and Performance Machine two-piston caliper. The 240-series rear tire is halted by an Exile Cycles sprotor and Performance Machine caliper, also a two-piston model.

Finishing off the build is a wide array of sheet metal collected from a number of sources. The fuel tank began life on an older British machine. Underneath, the tunnel was revised to sit differently on the frame. The upper surface was radically altered and now has the fuel filler at the forward-most point. The cap was taken from a 1920s Pontiac radiator.

The raised spine was another custom-made addition. It holds a dome light from a 1953 Olds Rocket in its contours. The light can be illuminated with the touch of a switch.

The House of Kolor Midnight Blue, layered with Silver Blue Metallic, is highlighted by two nose-art ladies for yet another touch of the old days. There's a blond on one side and a redhead on the other – both scantily yet tastefully clad. The Paint Spot applied the base hues, and Mike Olivera applied his handiwork to the female forms. The rear fender may have come from the Jesse James catalog but was modified by adding a fin from another 1950s car and molding the entire shape into the frame for a clean and uncluttered look.

With comfort far down the list of desired traits, the saddle offers no padding. It was handmade from bird's-eye maple, inlaid with another set of manually carved flames, and layered with acrylic for protection from the elements. A small leather cushion is provided for the small of Rich's back, but his posterior gets no such luxury.

The final surprise on Pyro's Woody is the small ball-peen hammer hanging in the circular rack. This bit of gang-related paraphernalia is meant to discourage passing motorists from pressuring the rider off the road. Perhaps not the most subtle method of warning other drivers, but it's all within the boundaries of Rich's handcrafted chopper.

Risers crafted by the builder were topped off with bird's-eye maple, and a pair of crystal knobs finishes off the springer front end.

Once found in the steering hub of a 1953 Oldsmobile, this piece has been relocated and does duty as the chopper's tail light now.

The ignition outlet is surrounded by another bit of yesteryear – a bottle opener.

RICH "PYRO" POLLACK

PYRO'S MEDIEVAL

Rich "Pyro" Pollack

ich "Pyro" Pollack spends a lot of time creating a vehicle in his mind before ever setting the wheels in motion. Pyro's Medieval may look like something he assembled over the weekend, but it took him an entire winter to complete. With a complete machine shop at his disposal and a high mechanical aptitude, Rich turns out many of his pieces by hand, adding another level of rarity to his creations. For this build, he wanted to do something in the David Mann style, which includes tall bars and clean yet classic design elements. As unfinished as it first appears, the raw steel finish and 30-inch ape hangers draw more attention than many of the high-dollar glossy bikes seen on

Rich "Pyro" Pollack and his Medieval machine.

television and in magazines. Regardless of how it's finished, the bike just looks cool, and people are drawn to that.

The chassis is a fairly straightforward edition from Harley and includes a 32-degree rake. No other changes were made to the length, height or lift. With the bike's raw, simple styling, Rich wanted to be sure it was well powered. For big power that is almost bullet-proof, he turned to John Kownacki, another Chicago firefighter who has a long-standing record of

building this type of motor. Most of the details of what went into the motor are trade secrets, but we do know the Evo engine breathes in through an Edelbrock carb and exhales with the help of short pipes from Paughco. A chrome Goodson air cleaner was detailed with some tasteful pinstriping, a theme that continues over the rest of the chopper. The factory tranny from Harley works with a primary from BDL and drives a chain to the rear sprocket-rotor unit.

Pounded from a sheet or two of raw steel, the finished tank stays raw and unprotected, just the way its builder wanted it.

Having a machine shop and talent allows a builder to turn out some amazing things. Rich spun out the forks and adjustable triple trees for this scoot, but they look like they were purchased from a catalog. A 60-spoke wheel carries a GMA rotor and caliper, and the aft rim revolves around 40 spokes. Another touch of Rich's genius can be found on the self-created foot pegs and controls. The perforated support legs find polished Maltese-cross pedals at the business end, which play a perfect role in this classic chopper design.

The 30-inch handlebars seem like an impossible reach, but they fit Rich's 6-foot, 8-inch physique perfectly. Grabbing onto the bars with one hand while shifting gears with the pointed-skull suicide lever is more than many riders can achieve. The ride is far from casual, but Rich enjoys the beast's raw nature. People also seem to appreciate his machine's base nature and riding style, especially when he sends the back wheel into a smoky burnout that goes on for days.

The Harley motor may look innocent, but it packs a punch when the throttle gets twisted.

The most striking features on Pyro's Medieval are the fender and fuel tank. Hammered from flat steel and left mostly unfinished, they draw more stares than some $5,000 paint schemes. The burnished look is not even protected by clear coat, and slight traces of rust have begun to add to the chopper's patina and magic. Look at almost any part of this bike and you'll find handmade items. Rich's hands crafted the drooping chain shift linkage and intricately detailed primary spider web. The web was first traced onto the steel and then cut with a common jigsaw before setting the file into motion for days on end. The result looks as if it's being pulled in several directions by the force of the primary belt. Even the belt is trimmed with the words "Pyro Chop" so people will know who built the thing, assuming that it sits still long enough for you to read it.

Lighting may be simple, but even the choices for these bits were tedious and well thought out. The Bates headlight is adorned with the handle from a fan, an item most of us would overlook as anything more than what it is. When combined with the small, chrome headlight bucket, it seems destined to go there. Another classic touch is the large Maltese-cross tail lamp covered with a wire mesh for added flare. These details set Rich's bikes apart from many others on the road today. The all-metal saddle, although lacking comfort, continues this build's raw nature, and the buffalo nickel encased in the primary is another detail not often seen. As seen on Pyro's Woody, a small ball-peen hammer is on duty to discourage any rude behavior from passing motorists. Even a light tap on the window can shatter glass.

Handmade triple trees are adjustable and hold a pair of turned fork legs, also handmade, within their grasp.

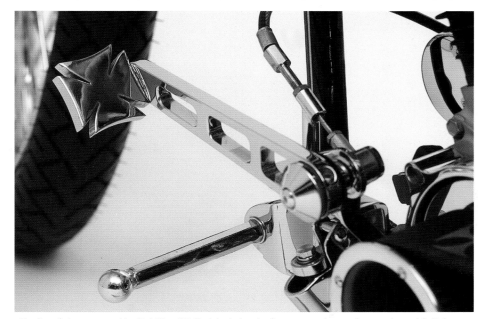

The list of pieces created by Rich "Pyro" Pollack includes the foot pegs and controls, complete with Maltese-cross pedals.

The intricate spider web represents hours of cutting, smoothing and filing before the chrome plating could be applied.

RUSSELL MARLOWE

HALF & HALF

Russell Marlowe

t has been many years since Russell Marlowe started messing around with motorcycles, but his interest, talent and customer base grew every day. After a while, it dawned on him that building choppers and working on others' machines could be a neat way to earn a living. After choosing bike builder as his occupation, he hung out his "Carolina Custom Cycles" shingle and went to work. The additional work brought more recognition and an invitation to enter the Heritage Motorcycle Rally Biker Build-Off. Dave Harvey organizes the event and offers a top prize of $100,000. Ten builders are invited to enter. The 2005 event yielded an amazing array of custom machines from a variety of builders. Some had appeared on the Discovery Channel's *Biker Build-Off*, but others lacked the same level of exposure. Regardless of who had been on television, entries for this event were nothing less than spectacular.

Not one to incorporate a lot of outside components on his one-of-a-kind builds, Russell began with a Phoenix chassis bearing his signature. The frame's most striking feature is the lack of a front down tube, which typically supports the motor and related hardware. By using the motor as a stressed member, the entire assembly stays rigid enough for daily use. The chassis' geometry is fairly radical and includes a rake of 50 degrees, kicking the forks way out in front. A stretch of 5 inches was

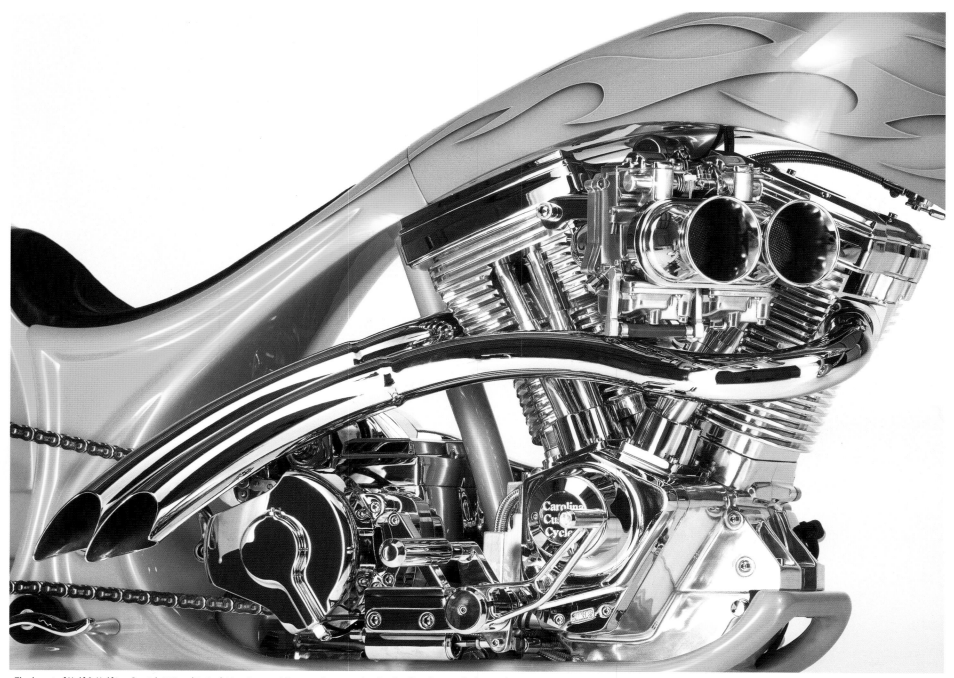

The heart of Half & Half is a Patrick 113-cubic-inch V-twin, providing ample power for the Carolina Custom Cycles machine.

added as well as another 8 inches over. Included in Russell's Phoenix chassis is a rear swing arm of his own creation. Progressive suspension components add some comfort to the equation, and a Perse FXSTC front fork is in charge of steering. The Perse forks are held in place by triple trees modified for this custom.

Providing the motivation is a 113-cubic-inch Patrick motor. J&E pistons ride within the Patrick cylinders, and S&S connecting rods keep them in check. S&S also provided the cases for the assembly, and a Mi-

kuni carburetor keeps the incoming blend consistent. A Crane ignition sparks the demon to life, and a set of Russell Marlowe pipes provides a graceful and efficient path for the departing exhaust.

Six speeds are included in the Primo transmission, and the same manufacturer was chosen for the clutch and primary assemblies. Final drive is via chain to allow room for the meaty 280-millimeter rear tire. Both polished rims began life as Metal Masters pieces and were altered for Half & Half. Metzler donuts keep everything rolling smoothly. HHI

The flowing fuel tank blends into the following bodywork. The handlebars are devoid of the usual cable and wire clutter.

A Progressive rear suspension delivers a smooth ride to the CCC-built swing arm and chassis.

A Primo transmission receives the power through a matching clutch and primary, and uses an open-belt design.

brake hardware is mounted to the front hoop, and the rear rim carries a combination of Exile Cycles and Russell Marlowe gear.

Every inch of the sweeping bodywork is Russell's doing, and he does it well. The fuel tank glides without a break into the seating area and continues on to the rear fender. The entire assembly is seamless but incorporates a few tasty body lines and sensuous contours to add some visual stimulation. Jimmy Lambert applied the DuPont Gold Pearl paint and

subtle flames. Additional Russell bits are found in the risers, handlebars, grips and hand controls. A 4 1/2-inch light from Headwinds shows the way at night, and a set of foot pegs and forward controls came from Billet 4-U. The minimalist saddle is another Marlowe original, with upholstery by David Sellers.

Along with the missing down tube, there are no exposed wires or throttle and clutch cables. Russell likes his choppers clean, and he cer-

tainly achieved that with Half & Half. Only 30 days were required to produce the machine, and Russell was pleased with the results.

How did the judges and public respond to his ultraclean machine? Half & Half took home the top honor at the 2005 Heritage Rally.

SCOTT PARKER SPECIAL

Echelon Motorcycles

After more than a decade of bike building, James Spiroff teamed up with Robert Brown to form Echelon Motorcycles. The firm was born right around the latest millennium's arrival and has grown to unforeseen proportions. Many of Echelon's clients return time and time again for new choppers, and this model was built for just such a customer.

Scott Parker plays for the San Jose Sharks hockey team and saw an opening in his garage that needed to be filled. As with all Echelon bikes, Scott went to the shop to be custom fitted for his new ride. By doing this, every bike fits the owner's physical traits like a well-made suit. Once the basic dimensions are taken, Echelon uses a computer-aided design system to lay out the chassis' geometry. Not only does Echelon build amazing, show-quality choppers, but each one can be ridden daily with confidence.

Echelon creates more than 40 percent of the components used in each machine. The frames, sheet metal and hard brake lines are in the company's catalog. All sheet metal is just that; no filler is used in creating the shapes. Powering Echelon choppers are the world's only billet mills, acquired from a firm named R&R. Billet is used on every motor component, including the cases. The term "bullet proof" comes to mind, and that's the intention of Echelon and R&R.

The all-billet V-twin is an R&R product. It is the only all-billet motor produced today.

With rider comfort one of its goals, Echelon chose from its inventory a chassis that comes complete with rear suspension. A 49-degree rake was matched with 18 over in the down tubes and a 4-inch stretch on the upper frame tube. These dimensions were determined by plugging the buyer's measurements into the CAD system, thus delivering a great looking frame that provides competent handling. The rear swing arm is another Echelon component and is mated to a Legends Air model L3 system. Front forks are from the Perse catalog and are an extra 18 inches long. Another 6 degrees of angle are gained by using Perse triple trees to hold the fork legs in place. Held in the front forks' grasp is a Triad wheel from Extreme Performance.

Metzeler ME880 rubber measures 3 1/4 inches by 21 inches and provides sure-footed traction and responsive handling. The matching front brake rotor also is a Triad model from Extreme Machines and is halted by a Performance Machine caliper.

The rear axle also carries a Triad wheel but has slightly larger dimensions than the front hoop. A 10-inch width is matched to an 18-inch diameter, and the 280-millimeter rear tire provides traction. Another matching triad brake disc is grabbed by a Performance Machine caliper. All brake lines were bent from hard line by Echelon and add another dimension of clean to the build.

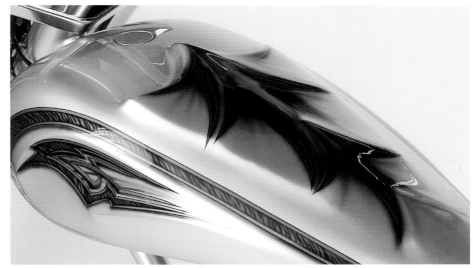

As if sporting body armor beneath its skin, the fuel tank was styled with contoured panels on the sides and top.

The chassis' single down tube was outfitted with a medieval-style detail that complements the rest of the paint and sheet metal.

The rear fender is another highly sculpted form. The paint only enhances the bike's theme.

The R&R motor displaces 127 cubic inches. The monster is fed by an S&S Super G carburetor. The Dual 300 ignition from Dyna delivers plenty of spark to keep things moving, and exhalation is completed through a Martin Bros. exhaust modified by Echelon. Baker sells a six-speed transmission that also is cut from billet, so it was the obvious choice for the all-billet mill. A Rivera clutch resists slippage, and the Billet 4-U primary transfers the power without fuss.

Echelon is responsible for the sheet metal, and the design looks a bit like the bike is wearing panels of body armor under the fuel tank's skin. The deeply contoured oil tank housing, seat pan and rear fender all blend together and appear to be a solid piece, complete with under-skin armor. Both fenders began their lives as Fat Katz pieces but received extensive alterations before being painted and installed. Stainless-steel lines for the oil tank also were done in tubing versus the usual soft-sided hose. The Spies-Hecker silver and black paint was applied with several areas of shading to augment the shapes formed in the sheet metal. Mike Learn was the trigger man on the paint's application.

The handlebars are another Echelon creation and sprout directly from the upper triple tree, avoiding the clutter of additional risers. Climax Custom Cycle grips complete the throttle, brake and clutch lever shopping list. Performance Machine Contour foot pegs and forward controls make beautiful places for the rider's boots to rest. A Headwinds light up front is joined by a taillight from Pro Fab and provides more than adequate wattage.

All wires, cables and hoses are hidden from view to maintain the chopper's super-clean look, and a custom-made starter cover completes the mission. It required six months of build time to complete, but the result was well worth the wait.

KNUCKLE SANDWICH

Pugliese Custom Cycles

As a kid growing up on Staten Island, N.Y., Michael Pugliese spent many hours at a local body shop, getting his first taste of working with metal and paint. Although he went on to become a construction contractor, his interest in motorcycles continued. His first exposure to building custom bikes came more than a decade ago when he bought a new Harley-Davidson Fat Boy and customized it. His satisfaction with the tricked-out Fat Boy led him to build his own chopper from the ground up. It's no mean feat for an experienced builder, but for a semipro, it was a daunting task.

The front end's 52-degree rake is kept under control by grabbing hold of the custom-made handlebars.

Working in his two-car garage until all hours of the night, Michael created his first chopper. For a guy with no formal training in the field, his debut effort won accolades among the media and public alike. This mark in the "win" column set off his quest to become one of the country's premier builders. Not long after his initial foray into custom bikes, he was a contestant on the Discovery Channel's Biker Build-Off. His burgeoning second career also led to an entry in the 2005 Heritage Motorcycle Rally Bike Build-Off in Charleston, S.C. One of only 10 builders invited to compete for the $100,000 top prize, Michael entered Knuckle Sandwich.

On many custom choppers, there's one primary feature that takes the crown for being the coolest or best engineered. On Knuckle Sandwich, there are quite a few. Once you get past the massive 360-millimeter rear tire and wheel, your eyes wander to the twin-spar frame. Each flank of the chassis begins at the swing-arm pivot and arches gracefully upward, joining forces at the rear of the fuel tank, which then becomes one with the frame. The curvature of the frame's front down tubes matches the curvature of the rear tresses to the letter. The overall effect is like a red metal flake bridge with an engine mounted within its expanse.

A single-sided swing arm is another technical wonder, especially considering the rear-tire width. The rim alone measures 14 inches across, nearly matching the 18-inch diameter of the chrome hoop provided by Performance Machine. Manufacturers of 360 rubber and rims are few and far between; they are seen on only a handful of bikes. Vee-Rubber made this acreage but also can provide more typical tires upon demand.

Chassis geometry also is quite radical, with a 52-degree rake at the steering head. Known to push the envelope of creativity, Michael also made the front forks in his shop instead of simply buying someone else's hardware. The springer forks are held at bay by Pugliese tubular triple trees. One bit of off-the-shelf componentry is the Progressive rear suspension, which keeps the mono-sided swing arm riding smoothly.

Nestled between the frame's twin spars is an Accurate Engineering Knucklehead mill displacing 103 cubic inches. With STD cases for the utmost in durability, it plays the role of a vintage Harley motor but is far stronger than the 1936 edition it mirrors. Blacked-out jugs are contrasted by highly polished heads and a raft of other shiny bits. Lineweber cams and an S&S Super E carb round out the lineup of power-plant players.

The crossed-over exhaust tubes were bent into submission by Michael in keeping with his hands-on way of working. A six-speed Baker transmission sends the power to the drive train via the Karata Enterprises clutch and a one-off primary designed exclusively for Knuckle Sandwich. To select the desired gear, you pull in the clutch and grab the chromed set of brass knuckles that reaches up between the frame rails. "Normal" may not be in Michael's vocabulary, but we are all better off for that.

Reaching the drive-train part of the tour, we find yet another technical masterpiece from Michael's creative mind. A typical chain or belt drive would have caused a number of alignment or layout difficulties. To avoid those troubles and set the chopper world on its ear, Michael drafted a friction drive onto his bike. A rubber drive wheel contacts the rear rubber to rotate the massive donut. Not only does this system work, but the layout allows the bike to perform huge, smoky burnouts with little perceived effort. Any naysayers of the friction drive are quickly quieted by the blinding wall of smoke pouring from the rear tire.

So now we know how the bike goes, but how does it stop? There's no sign of a disc brake on either of the Performance Machine rims, but there must be some form of mechanical braking, right? Yes, there is, but again, it is probably nothing you've seen before. Mounted to the end of the shaft that drives the friction wheel is a disc brake from Performance

The only braking available to the rider is this Performance Machine disc that lives on the end of the friction drive shaft.

Front forks of Michael Pugliese's creation are complete with these chrome springs to bring a bit of compliance to the chassis.

▶ The 103-cubic-inch Knucklehead mill is finished with black jugs and highlights of chrome, making the perfect statement in this design.

Machine. The rotor's action is stopped by a P.M. caliper and is the only way of slowing the bike down, regardless of what velocity you may have attained. It certainly is not the strongest braking system in the known world, but it is one of the coolest and best engineered.

The only sheet metal on this creation is the fuel tank, and its execution and design are flawless. Even the tank's smooth underside is enclosed, providing an uncluttered view from any angle. Michael created the tank, once again showing us that he really does know how to put one of these things together. A tiny saddle is covered in a combination of shark skin and black leather, bringing a touch of the exotic to the techni-

cal tour de force. Handlebars, foot pegs, and shifting and braking controls also are Pugliese components. He did turn to the parts catalog for a few minor bits, such as the CCI headlight and Lamberts taillight. Performance Machine also is guilty as charged for supplying the handgrips. Flawless candy-red paint is trimmed with segments of tribal flames in several shades of silver.

Only the smallest of mechanical glitches kept Michael's machine from taking home the bacon at the Heritage Bike Build-Off, but his creation remains at the top of its class in the crowded field of custom choppers. The only question I have: What does he do for an encore?

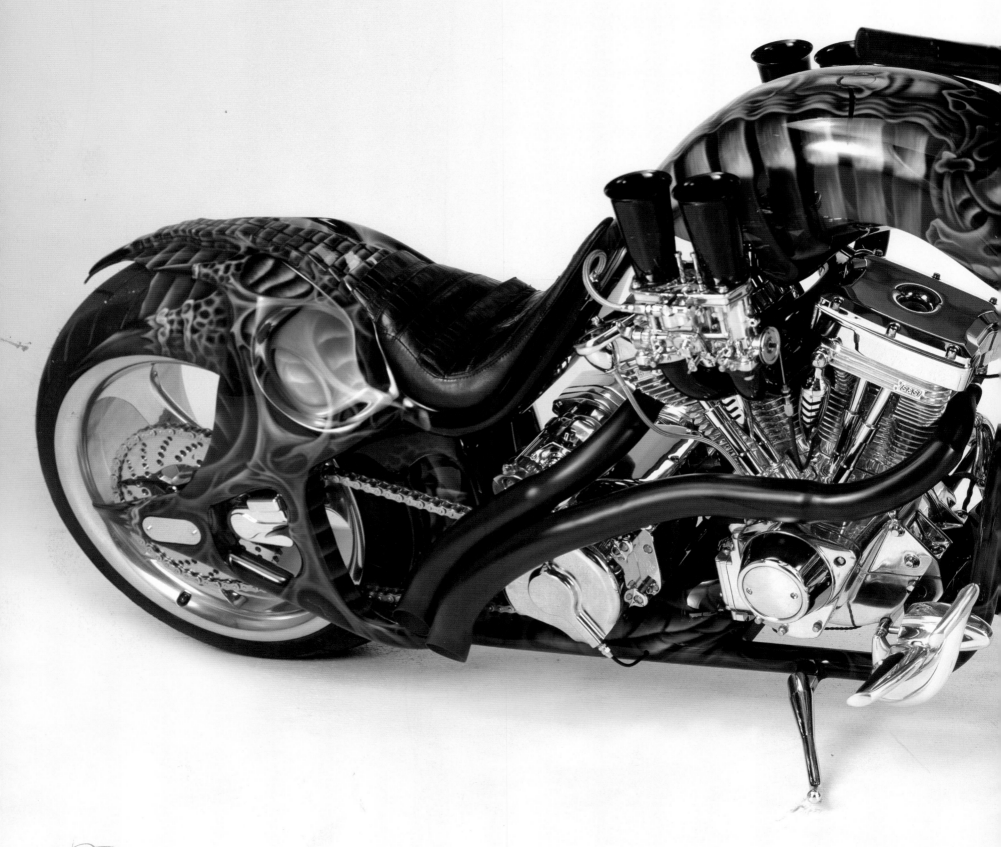

RESURRECTION

Mad Creations Custom Cycles

Anyone interested in custom motorcycles is aware of the many theme bikes that have been built. Subjects have included super heroes, farm implements, movies, and even a giant cheeseburger. Most have used primarily paint and graphics to carry the concept. Mad Creations Custom Cycles took its theme bike several steps further and incorporated custom sheet metal to create a convincing Alien replica. Named Resurrection after one of the movies in the series, this monster lives to terrorize those of us on the street, not aboard a space-bound craft. The movie creature was inspired by the art of H.R. Giger, whose work is a mix of macabre and intense details. Viewing any number of his pieces brings your imagination to attention and likely some disturbing dreams to your slumber.

MCCC officially opened in October 2003 but had already amassed many years of bike-building experience before taking that big step. Once it decided to build a chopper in the mold of the space creature, MCCC knew that simply painting the monster onto a set of fenders and tank would present enough of a statement about its abilities as a custom-bike builder. Bend-

ing and shaping the sheet metal into the required form wouldn't be easy, but would prove that the shop was worthy of being listed among the best. Some consider theme bikes kind of cheesy, so MCCC realized any effort in this medium would need to be top notch with no holds barred.

Beginning with a chassis from Brighton Frame Werks, the mission took off. Choosing a rigid frame would earn MCCC a bit more respect from the tried and true riders, and the 45-degree rake would keep the shop in good standing with contemporary standards. A 6-inch stretch made some extra room for the soon-to-be-crafted ornate tank that would ride on the upper tube. Forks, along with triple trees to hold them in place, were brought in from Arlen Ness and were trimmed by 2 inches to maintain a higher level of handling. The single-down-tube frame was augmented

The saddle's exotic upholstery sits just in front of the rear fender, which is a mix of compound curves and disturbing graphics.

with the first of two talons at the tube's lower extremity.

Nested between the fork tubes is an all-steel fender that is a highly detailed replica of the alien head seen in the movie. Weighing nearly 60 pounds, it is a prodigious piece of steel but really brings a high level of visual punch to the concept. Not only are the jaws and teeth formed to include a high level of detail, but the MCCC paint work brings the level of accuracy to new heights. The result of these efforts is a three-dimensional demon that encompasses most of the front wheel and tire.

Eurocomponent rims and Metzeler rubber were chosen for Resurrection. The sheet metal's amazing level of detail almost makes the wheels and tires afterthoughts, but the package does an admirable job of keeping the beautifully painted frame rails off the ground. Topping off the front

forks and triple trees are set-off molded handlebars created by MCCC. The gusset between the Southern Machine grips presents another panel for detailed airbrush work, and the builders wasted no time in using the space to their advantage.

The next expanse of custom sheet metal is found on the equally ornate and detailed fuel tank. The steeply arched creation appears poised to pounce as it blends from the down tubes to the saddle. The entire unit was created from scratch and required many hours of shaping. The flowing, muscular contours are covered with airbrush art that does H.R. Giger proud. Every square inch of steel on this bike is covered with the creature's imagery and carries the theme to the fullest. The drop saddle is an Advanced Seat Design creation and is covered in a combination of alligator

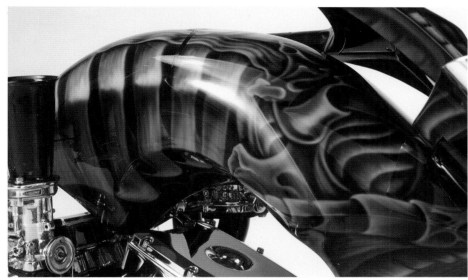

The arched fuel tank lies in wait for its next unsuspecting victim.

The second of two talons is found at the rear fender and is again highlighted by the detailed paint.

An S&S motor powers Resurrection and is fitted with a hand-bent set of tubes from Mad Creations Custom Cycles.

and sting-ray pelts. Another Brighton Frame Werks bit is found beneath the saddle, and it holds the required lubricants in a modified housing.

Reaching the rear fender, we find another handcrafted chunk of steel. "Chunk," however, isn't appropriate because of the compound contours and highly detailed sheet metal involved in the creation. A trio of talons reaches over and around the 280-millimeter rear tire, and the piece's remaining lines are graceful, yet menacing. Adding to the contradiction is more immensely detailed artwork covering the rear cowl. Regardless of

how much time you spend viewing this chopper, you'll always find a new detail you missed earlier.

No matter how amazing the bodywork may be, a chopper is nothing without power, and Resur-

rection doesn't disappoint. Displacing 107 cubic inches, the S&S twin is polished and provides a nice contrast to the dark and moody sheet metal. A single carburetor would have done an adequate job of feeding the mill, but MCCC wanted to add another dimension of terror to the drive train. Fitted with a matching set of vertically mounted Webers, each drawing breath through four blacked-out velocity stacks, the motor also steps into another dimension.

A pair of swept-back exhaust tubes from MCCC completes the functional aspect of this two-wheeled sculpture.

Forward speeds are listed at six and are provided by the Baker transmission. Hi-Tech delivers the clutch and primary, and a chain meets with a K-Tech rear sprotor. This unit is stopped by a caliper of the same maker, and front brakes are a combo platter of Eurocomponents rotor and Performance Machine caliper.

Considering how much raw creation and detailed paint work was required, the claimed two-month production seems a miracle. Perhaps a being from another world aided the project. Only Mad Creations Custom Cycles knows for sure.

THE BOOBY TRAP

Chopsmiths Inc.

Jason Hart and his Chopsmiths Inc. may be fairly new to chopper building, but their handmade cycles have already appeared in several major books and periodicals. In a universe chocked full of builders, that is not an easy achievement. One of the many reasons for their success is the innovative components used on each machine. You won't find many catalog parts on their bikes, except for tires and maybe a frame. Even when an off-the-shelf part is used, it's heavily modified before installation.

Jason's goal in building bikes is to include old-world parts with today's cutting-edge hardware and technology. You won't find flashy graphics, wild paint or lots of chrome on a Chopsmiths bike. You will find unusual bits and pieces from a variety of unorthodox sources, all used imaginatively. Jason had no reason for naming

Jason Hart, founder of Chopsmiths Inc., sits astride his latest creation, The Booby Trap.

his latest scoot The Booby Trap, but the creativity used to build it supersedes any moniker a person can come up with.

Taking a bit of inspiration from Hank Young, another prominent builder of unusual choppers, Jason began this project with a frame from Independent Cycle. The Low Life chassis was then highly altered. The most obvious change was the 1929 Ford Model A axle that replaced the factory top tube. Chopsmiths' creations often use automotive components, but most are not as obvious as the perforated spine borrowed from the an-

tique Ford. Chassis geometry is fairly tame, carrying only 40 degrees of rake and a mild stretch from adding the car axle.

Chopsmiths builds some unusual stuff, but everything the shop builds can and is ridden – hard. Not willing to sacrifice comfort for cool, The Booby Trap rides on a Legend Air rear suspension, which provides seamless and adjustable ride height. Redneck Engineering pro-

Residing beneath an axle from a 1929 Ford Model A is a hand-formed fuel tank created in aluminum-kilned steel.

vided the sprung front fork, but it, too, was modified before installation. The fork's top tubes were drilled to match the through-holes of the Model A axle. To maintain structural integrity and enhance the mechanical detailing, tube serts were welded into each orifice in the fork. This provides a clean opening that keeps dirt and debris out of the tubes.

Triple trees also hail from Redneck Engineering. They were mated with Independent Cycle handlebars that received the Chopsmiths' touch before being attached. A set of Chopsmiths Wooden Nickle grips finished off the bars with a surprising touch of hardwood. Brake and clutch levers were also created from scratch by Chopsmiths. Trademark components on Chopsmiths' machines are head and taillights built from old vehicle pistons. Leading the way is a Pistalite that was machined to hold the lamp and lens in perfect orientation yet allows for easy bulb replacement or adjustment. The brake light was fashioned from an ironhead Sportster piston and was mounted to the frame with an automotive door hinge.

Slung beneath the Model A axle is a hand-formed fuel tank. Only hard work and time – no wooden bucks or other system – were used to shape the aluminum-kilned steel. Despite the absence of a buck, the tank appears symmetrical to the naked eye, and that's really all that matters. The Light Quasar Blue Metallic paint is accented by the vintage "V2" logo applied to each side of the tank. An alloy fuel cap tops off the tank. Holding the oil in check is another Low Life item from Independent Cycles. The rear fender, hammered out in aluminum, was the final section of sheet metal formed by Chopsmiths. Again, no buck was used to

The Pistalite, a Chopsmiths creation, is made by joining an automotive piston with a modern bulb and lens to light your way at night.

Redneck Engineering triple trees are trimmed with ornate pinstriping to accent and highlight the otherwise mundane components.

earn the contours, just hours of raw labor and a keen eye for detail.

The best sheet metal in the world does a chopper rider no good without a motor, and for that, Chopsmiths turned to several suppliers to create another original. S&S cases hold a set of 88-cubic-inch jugs in place, providing the Keith Black pistons a well-honed home. S&S connecting rods keep the slugs in step, and STD valves and heads provide adequate breathing. Leinweber cams keep the valves in lockstep with the motor's other internal factions. External oil lines were added to the revised cylinder heads to provide lubrication to the now separated segments of each head.

A single, dual-throat Del'Orto carb was finished off with stubby, black velocity stacks. A Carne HI-4 ignition fires the works to life, and a pair

of hand-bent exhaust tubes are wrapped with heat tape for looks and performance. A six-speed gearbox from Accessories Unlimited sends the chosen ratio through a Primo clutch and modified Independent Cycles primary. Final drive is by chain, complete with a tensioner to keep things tight.

Gear selection is accomplished by grabbing the alloy knob that rests atop the

lengthy, drilled lever assembly, which sprouts from the power plant's left side. Rolling stock comes in the form of Metzeler rubber mounted to altered R.C. Components rims. With no sign of brakes on the front wheel, the scrap-yard rotor out back is pinched by a four-piston caliper from Performance Machine. A sparsely padded pillion was mounted to a leaf spring to provide a modicum of comfort. The official Chopsmiths branding was hand tooled into the rough and rugged surface.

The Booby Trap follows closely on the heels of Shovelglide and the AstroZombie, both of which started Chopsmiths on the way to a well-earned reputation for building bizarre, yet functional, two-wheeled art. As with all builders, this art can be added to your gallery for the right price. Let the bidding begin.

200 PROOF

BREW Bikes LLC

Steve "Brew Dude" Garn owns and operates a company that produces high-end, lightweight bicycle frames. Operating under the corporate heading BREW Bikes LLC, Steve's BREW Racing Frames builds some of the finest frames available. This passion has been growing since the early 1970s, when Steve began building frames to finance his motocross racing. (He ranked third in the 125

class in 1974.) As his bicycle efforts progressed, so did his desire to ride motorcycles on and off the track. His racing days may be through, but his interest in riding and building remains strong today.

Steve wanted to build a true example of an old-school chopper, so nothing but a bobber would do. He liked the simple styling it represented and the clean design of the period machines. Today's market is full of

A true-to-life, 74-cubic-inch Panhead motor from Harley-Davidson powers 200 Proof and is complete with the original Linkert carb.

retro frames that mimic vintage rides, but Steve followed the true old-school path. To begin, he chose a Harley-Davidson chassis and converted the sprung frame into a rigid. There was no alteration to the rake, length or geometry, but an updated front end was employed to aid handling. With intentions of having a scoot that looked great but was a bit firmer up front, Steve harvested a 2002 Triumph Bonneville for its fork assembly, thus bringing modern steering to the vintage-looking machine.

For the engine, Steve again could have selected one of today's modern mills, but opted for a 74-cubic-inch Panhead from the Milwaukee maker. Hoping to keep things as original as possible, he returned the Linkert carburetor to duty when building 200 Proof. A BREW-produced air cleaner brings a hint of modern to the otherwise antique mount, but not enough to spoil the fun. Even Harley's factory-installed ignition was used, but an exhaust from Paughco was installed for freer breathing. The semimatte

Black wrinkle paint is highlighted by bright ribs on the motor's case.

The twin pipes from Paughco wind their way to the back of the chassis, where they turn out and up for an easy exit.

An old-world kick-start lever is mated to an equally old-world Maltese-cross pedal.

Flat, drag-style handlebars are complete with a single instrument and handmade brass-knuckle mirror mounts.

black pipes snake their way to the chassis' rear, where they take a subtle turn upward and away.

The kick-start lever, complete with Maltese-cross pedal, is still used to fire up the 74. Most choppers built for the current market feature six- or seven-speed gearboxes, but 200 Proof sticks with the tried and true four-speed from Harley. A newer BDL primary, however, helps the transition between motor and transmission.

A bare minimum of sheet metal was used to build the bike. The fuel tank and rear trailer fender are from Paughco. The tank doesn't hold a ton of fuel, but provides enough mileage to get around town at a respectable speed. The black powder-coated frame is nicely matched by the black and metallic sparkle blue hues applied to the sheet metal. Steve at BREW applied the PPG paint. A simple bit of orange pinstripe, added by Dan Kite, separates the two hues and is also seen on various chassis tubes.

A simple yet timely black and blue paint scheme is divided by a solitary orange stripe and looks right at home, even in today's world of high-end customs.

The solo saddle is upholstered in metal flake blue to match the hue applied to the fuel tank and fender.

Dunlop Qualifier rubber rolls at both ends, with a 110-millimeter between the forks and a 130-millimeter at the drive chain. Nothing more than spoke wheels were permitted on this scoot. A Triumph unit mounted between the fork tubes provides lighting, and a BREW custom taillight indicates a slowing bike from behind. BREW is also responsible for the brass-knuckle mirrors, foot controls and handlebars. The only instrumentation is the circular speedometer and odometer mounted to the drag-style bars. The tiny one-person saddle was covered in speedboat metal flake blue by Leatherworks, matching the paint, and is suspended by a tiny shock absorber of its own. The seat is another bit of BREW technology, looking like something from the past.

In creating 200 Proof, Steve Garn built a real-world machine that reeks of old-world charm.

BREW BIKES LLC

RIDGE RUNNER

BREW Bikes LLC

With a wealth of frame building know-how and a desire to build a modern bobber, Steve Garn turned to the Buell brand for a start. A 2001 model was sacrificed for the project, and the result is a far cry from what Harley-powered bikes on showroom floors offer.

With sport-bike buyers in mind, the Buell chassis is well designed and delivers terrific performance. Wanting more of a chopper stance, Steve took the Buell frame and trashed all but one tube before creating a new platform for Ridge Runner. The new math holds the front forks at a more extreme 34-degree rake, an increase of 9 over the stock dimension.

A BREW air cleaner keeps the 145-horsepower motor breathing nicely.

Kustomwerks provided the fuel tank, and the dark blue paint is accented by silver leaf tribal flames.

Three inches of height was removed from the factory trim and got the machine down to better fighting weight. Of course, no true bobber would be caught dead with rear suspension, so Ridge Runner is another rigid example roaming the streets. The remaining chassis components, such as the front forks, are carryovers from the Buell.

The Sportster motor displaces 1,203 cc's directly from the assembly line, and that number was retained. A BREW air cleaner was added to enhance breathing, as was a custom exhaust canister at the end of factory pipes. Another small modification was made to the engine by adding a Pingel nitrous-oxide delivery system. By spraying a small dose

A nitrous system provides boost to the Buell's 1,203-cc power plant.

Lighting the road at night are a pair of high-intensity halogen head lamps.

Adding a touch of old world to the modern Ridge Runner is a vintage 1930s Harley tail light.

The single front rotor is massive and taken right off the Buell parts shelf.

The minimalist saddle was upholstered by Steve Garn, showing his talent goes beyond metal and motors.

of nitrous into the cylinders, horsepower grows from 115 to 145 at the touch of a button. Can you say "fun" and "wheelie?" I knew you could. Combined with a lower wet weight of only 431 pounds, a serious gain in overall performance was achieved.

Performance Machine wheels were installed on both axles, and Dunlop donuts keep them shiny. The front rim is devoid of any fender in keeping with the beast's bobber nature. The enormous Buell brake rotor also was retained and needs nothing to increase its functionality.

The rear fender and fuel tank are Kustomwerks components, and the fuel tank's underside was modified by BREW before installation on this street fighter. The drum-shaped, stainless-steel oil tank is another BREW component and looks right at home on this new millennium bobber. The paint scheme is straightforward and includes silver tribal flames on a field of blue. Bobbers of days past typically wore simple colors with little ornamentation, so a flashy paint job on this contemporary example just wouldn't seem right.

Steve and his son routinely tool around town and events aboard their well-built machines, such as 200 Proof. The bikes often draw attention because of their low-key appearance, gaining points for originality and perfect execution.

JAW DROPPER

Kingpin Cycles

Jaw Dropper is the latest machine to roll out of Kingpin Cycles' shop in Corpus Christi, Texas. Other builds have included Low Class, Fat Daddy, The Deuce, and Dr. Feelgood. First-place trophies and People's Choice and Editor's Choice awards decorate Kingpin's showroom.

The massive 127-cubic-inch motor was assembled using only race-quality hardware for bone-crunching power and durability.

Jaw Dropper was built around an RPM 127-cubic-inch motor filled with the highest performance components available. Ross pistons are carried by Carrillo connecting rods, and both travel in Ultima cylinders. Manly valves are controlled by Andrews cams, and RPM-Ultima heads keep the lid tight. A Davinci Model 6 carburetor monitors the air and fuel flow, and a Spyke Dual Fire ignition sets the blend to fire. Rapidly moving gases are expelled through a Kingpin two-into-one exhaust system finished in deep chrome. Putting all of this power to the street is a Road Max six-speed transmission teamed with a top-fuel primary from BDL. A BDL clutch makes the transition from stop to top speed smooth.

All of the go-fast hardware is bolted onto a Big Poppa chassis from The Wrench. The 45- degree rake is paired with another 6 inches of stretch in the top tube and 2 inches added to the down tube. A single-sided swing arm from War Eagle leaves the rear wheel's right side exposed, showing the RC Components Wicked wheel, which features a separate spinner for some added bling. A matching front rim rides within the 21-inch by 3 1/4-inch Avon Venom tire. The rear tire measures 18 inches by 250 millimeters and provides a solid footprint for the motor's output.

Keeping the rear tire planted is an air-ride suspension from Tricky. Adjustable ride height and stiffness provide the rider flexibility and comfort.

The spinner rim's right side is open and available for our viewing pleasure, while the left side carries the rotor and hidden caliper.

Ron Peck and his Kingpin crew.

Triple trees from American Suspension hold the Phantom front forks in place and add another 6 degrees of angle to the mix. Adding 8 inches to the smooth fork legs gave Jaw Dropper an aggressive, yet usable, stance. Incorporated into the fork's left leg is an invisible brake caliper, which provides a laboratory-clean look while delivering ample stopping power. The front wheel is another Wicked model and is matched by a rotor of the same name.

Another trick up Kingpin's sleeve is the drive-side pulley brake that combines both components into a single unit and slows the chopper safely. Having a full toy box allows Kingpin to include some innovative features, and the air-operated center stand is one of the coolest. No need to kick out the usual side stand or struggle with getting the weight onto a typical center stand. With the touch of a button, the stands drops down and supports the machine without fuss.

The Wrench was the primary source for sheet metal. It is responsible for the soft tail, hidden oil bag, and both fenders, which Kingpin reconfigured. An Independent Tormentor fuel tank was stretched 10 inches by Kingpin to fill the frame's elongated top tube. A full-quill ostrich saddle cradles the rider's hindquarters in style and a bit of comfort. Reaching back to the rider's grasp is a set of pull-back bars from The Wrench, which were accented with Spyke grips from RPM.

A tasteful and dramatic paint scheme finished off this 10-month build. Oriental Blue Kandy trimmed with Orion Silver and Neon Green paint from House of Kolor sealed the deal. Auto Crafters technicians were the guys with the gun.

With an already impressive list of accolades to its credit and a tool belt full of tricks, it will be interesting to see what Kingpin unleashes next on the chopper market.

DINO'S CUSTOM CYCLES

Many people in the motorcycle business were infected with the desire to ride soon after they threw a leg over anything with two wheels. Some didn't even require the object to have a motor; others were lucky to have a small minibike or similar contrivance to get the disease. Regardless of your experience, we all share the same taste of adventure that riding a motorcycle brings.

Ruben Guerra was no different. His first ride, at age 10, ignited a steadily burning fire within. It would be many years before he was able to fan the flames and start building choppers. His first foray into the cycle market was selling parts to other bike builders, but a short year later he began to construct his own machine. It has been nearly a decade since his first parts shop opened, but Dino's Custom Cycles has gone far in the short run.

An annual show in Denver offered stiff competition among private owners of custom choppers, but Ruben and some other builders thought it unfair for the shops to compete against the people who bought bikes and parts from them. This conflict led to a build-off among those who crafted the machines, and in the first year, Ruben's Chop DeVille took home the top honor. The only people invited back for another year of fun were those who won, so Ruben returned with Twisted the following year and won again.

Dino's Custom Cycles participated in the 2005 Heritage Motorcycle Rally in Charleston, S.C., and was invited to enter Heritage's $100,000 build-off in 2006. July 2005 also earned Twisted another top honor, at the Buffalo Run build-off held in Miami, Okla. Judging was a mix of popular vote and judge's review. Seven builders pitted their best in a competition to take home the big prize. Chosen to judge the 2005 event was none other than Russell Mitchell of Exile Cycles. His history is well documented, and two of his creations are shown in this book.

Hardly a high-production builder, Dino's has assembled maybe 25 bikes since it started, but each one is a new view on a two-wheeled theme. Most of his bikes are built to meet a customer's desires, but Ruben often ends up selling bikes he's building for himself because of demand from a hungry audience. From what we've seen so far, we have a lot to look forward to, as Dino's Custom Cycles continues to turn out some unique choppers.

TWISTED

Dino's Custom Cycles

From a distance of, say, a mile or so, Twisted may not appear to be all that radical a build. Any distance less than that reveals amazing attention to detail and metal contorted into shapes it wasn't meant to have. Perhaps the most obvious use of tortured steel is the chassis' backbone. Scotty's Choppers provided the basic form, but Dino's used a high-pressure machine to twist the solid steel bar into the shape we see here. Slung beneath the

tube is a fuel tank formed from scratch in Dino's shop. The top section's gentle curve is contrasted by the radically contoured insets at the piece's front. A beautifully sculpted fuel cap keeps a lid on the precious contents within and adds another dimension of detail. For the tech fan, there's even a small monitor attached to a rear-mounted camera that can be used whenever you need to see who you just passed.

To some, the twirling front forks may be the first things they notice when approaching Twisted. The primary supports were formed from larger-diameter bar stock and painted, but the upper lengths are a smaller diameter and chrome plated. The springs allow for some front-end movement. The Dino's-created triple trees, which would look right at home in the Bat Cave, keep the forks in their required location. A set of Perse

handgrips formed from hollow stock are mounted to the bars, another bit of Dino's genius.

The frame's tail end carries a Scotty's Choppers swing arm and is suspended by a custom application of a Tricky Air system. Not only does the swing arm carry the rear wheel and drive sprocket, but it holds the required lubrication for the motor, thus saving the space usually taken by the oil bag. The Twisted Tribal rear fender is yet another chunk of Dino's creativity, which seems to be boundless. It's hardly capable of stopping much rainwater from reaching your back, but it looks great anyway.Bitchen Stitchen takes credit for the black leather upholstery we find on the typically small saddle made for one.

Cradled in the twisted steel frame is a 113-cubic-inch V-twin from RPM. Adding another level of visual appeal is the diamond-cut cool-

Replacing the typical bar-mounted mirrors is a back-up camera, which can be monitored on this small video screen.

The rear sprotor was engraved with Dino's corporate logo. The frame rails are trimmed with a pointed bit of polished metal for show.

◄ The exhaust pipes sprouting from the side of the RPM 113-cubic-inch motor resemble coiled pythons.

Holding the fork legs and handlebars in place are custom triple trees from Dino's.

ing fins on the cylinders. A dual Weber carb rides high on the end of an upswept intake and is finished off by a Streamline Deluxe air cleaner. Flanking the intake system is a pair of Dino's Twisted Up exhaust. Their shape is reminiscent of a python poised to strike at anyone passing too close. Ignition is caused by a Crane HI-4 arrangement. Six speeds are at the rider's avail, provided by the RPM gearbox mated with a Kenny Boyce clutch and primary.

Chrome hoops at both ends are Barbed models

from Metal Monster. The trailing rubber measures 300 millimeters wide. Avon Venom keeps the shiny rims safe from the evil pavement. The only braking present on Twisted is the rear sprotor from Exile Cycles. As we've seen on other choppers, this unit combines the drive sprocket and rear rotor into a single component, saving space and weight.

Twisted's paint is from House of Kolor and includes Candy Apple Red, Orion Silver and Black to create the subtle shading and intricately detailed ensemble of colors.

CHOP DEVILLE

Dino's Custom Cycles

C hop DeVille is Dino's Custom Cycle's first build-off winner. It set the stage for subsequent victories at a number of competitions across the country. Twirled steel tubes are Twisted's focal point, but on this example, we find a different set of rules being broken.

The tour starts at the heavily sculpted DeVille fuel tank with deeply concave side panels that take a moment for the eye to grasp. The side-panel insets contrast starkly to the tank's almost perfectly flat top section. Colorful graphics, including a bit of gold leaf in the tribal flames on the upper surface, add to the surfaces' dimensions. The sheet-metal parade continues with an oil bag that began life as a Paramount item. It was stretched and molded to morph into what we see here. The new shape engulfs the vertical and lower frame tubes into its seamless vortex of shape.

Some tiny gold-leaf flames also lick the surface of this compound curve.

Looking to either end of Chop DeVille, we find Fat Katz fenders that were cut into three-dimensional flames, then painted to accent the careful incisions. Beneath the front fender lies a chrome spoke wheel, complete with an inner spinner that rotates freely. These multiaction wheels are Dino's originals and add movement even when the chopper is standing still. The rear fender also hides a copy of Dino's spinner-spoke wheel, this one fitted to a 280-series donut from Avon.

Continuing the sheet metal's visual appeal are the highly detailed cuts that created the rear fender's flames.

Flames cut into the primary cover are joined by the engraved Dino's logo, taking detailing to the extreme.

The fuel tank's deeply sculpted sides reduce capacity but increase the visual excitement.

A Paramount soft-tail frame gives this custom sheet metal a good home. The 45-degree rake is joined by another 6 inches over and 4 inches out in the layout. Legend Air tames the rear swing arm, also from Paramount. Compliance up front is created by a Goldammer G-Force fork that was stretched 10 inches. Unlike 99 percent of the choppers seen in magazines or on the street, Chop DeVille uses no triple trees to hold the forks in place. The Goldammer unit mounts directly to the steering head, and risers sprout from there. The risers on this example sweep toward the rider and become the handlebars, creating a clean transition from fork to grips.

When you ride with this much style, an excess of displacement isn't required. A 96-cubic-inch RPM motor rides in the chassis and delivers plenty of forward motion when required. Of course, a turbocharger mounted to the V-twin's side also helps. A Spike air cleaner keeps debris out before the air is forced into the motor via the turbo and S&S carb. Dino's Turbo-X exhaust combines two outlets into one, which snakes through the bodywork and exhales through a gaping maw of an opening.

Although somewhat diminished in displacement, the S&S carburetor is force fed by the turbocharger, more than making up for any lack of size.

The enormous exit of the two-into-one exhaust resides here, looking every bit as evil as a cave-dwelling eel from the sea.

This system forces air into the motor and poses no restrictions on the way out.

All this power would be nothing without gears, so six are provided in the RPM tranny. A clutch from Barnett's and a BDL primary transfer power to the rear-pulley and brake-rotor combination from Leo's Customs. The primary cover was cut into the detailed flame scheme and engraved with the Dino's logo.

Part of the four months required to complete the build was used to apply the multiple colors and amazing details in the graphics. A flow of red, orange and yellow created the graduated color scheme accented by bits of gold leaf and a pearlescent top coat. The black leather seat is another item from Bitchen Stitchen.

One lucky man owns Twisted and Chop DeVille, and we can only hope he allows someone else a chance to buy the next multiple-award winner created by Dino's Custom Cycles.

CLEAR AND PRESENT DANGER

Jerry Burrows

J erry Burrows is another builder whose roots run deep in the custom-cycle community and are reaching further than imagined by him and his crew. As with many of today's well-known builders, Jerry started his lunacy with a 1966 Harley-Davidson Sportster that needed some attention. By combining restoration and customization, he created his first personalized bike, and the race was on.

Things started slowly, but he soon outgrew his cramped work space and moved into a 10,000-square-foot building. The new space allowed him to really flex his wings and enter a higher level of building. Along with building full-blown customs, Jerry's Road-Hawgs shop sells a wide array of parts and offers a knowledgeable service department that addresses Harleys of all ages. This aspect of his business gets a high priority. Riders of the older machines are having trouble finding dealers who are even capable of servicing the older models, let alone interested.

Jerry's lengthy history of building show-winning machines got him invited to the 2005 Heritage Motorcycle Rally Bike Build-Off in Charleston, S.C. Up against nine other of the country's best builders, Jerry knew the competition would be stiff. The results were extremely close, with another builder taking home the big prize, but Road-Hawgs got some valuable exposure and a chance to show off its talents in the South. Any ink is good ink, or so they say, and Clear and Present Danger gained some new fans and well-earned respect.

An enormously strong ladder-style frame section holds the rear tire in place.

◄ The 113-cubic-inch Patrick V-twin provides Clear and Present Danger with all the energy it needs, even with the gargantuan 360-millimeter rear tire.

Virtually every square inch of Clear and Present Danger bristles with innovation and ingenious new ways of doing old things. The build's foundation is a Jackshaft frame of Road-Hawgs design and construction. A serious 55-degree rake was thrown into the chassis length, which exceeds most seen on today's offerings. Exile Cycles' Massive Glide forks and triple trees are more than capable of steering this limousine of motorcycles without difficulty, regardless of the crazy angle at the steering head. Certain aspects of this chopper are fresh ideas, but a rear suspension was not an option. Maybe the old-school training burned into Jerry's brain just won't let him go.

The sensuous shape of the Cool fuel tank is another Road-Hawgs piece and is adorned with a chrome beak that draws the eye's attention away from the metallic black paint. Just behind the tank's trailing edge, the V-twin's rear cylinder juts out between splayed frame tubes and shows off its transparent cylinder head cover. These items were formed from a material that is similar to bullet-proof glass and difficult to machine into a shape as complex as we see here. Other components on Clear and Present Danger were milled from the same material.

The saddle was built from a metal pan instead of fiberglass because Jerry finds it easier to work with steel in this department. The cover was

Mounted to the frame's front down tube is another item formed from the same transparent material used on the cylinders.

At a fork in the frame, the rear cylinder head rears up and makes it obvious.

The polished motor breathes deeply through the Davinci carburetor, which hangs out in the airflow via an extended intake.

hand stitched and embossed by Jerry and Hi-End. Following the path backward, we find a rear fender that blends fluidly into the chassis' lower section and rear wheel support. Coated in the same metallic black as the fuel tank, it takes on a sinewy and sensuous nature. The brake light also is integrated into the shape for a seamless and safe application.

The rear ladder's substantial construction was required to maintain structural rigidity when applying the juice to the 360-millimeter rear rubber. Another unique facet of this design is the rear wheel rim, which was created from the same transparent material seen on the cylinders. The wheel's central section was taken from a Metal Monsters wheel and more

readily allows for the use of axle bearings. This construction's durability was proven when Jerry took Clear and Present Danger on the 40-mile ride required by the Heritage Build-Off. Not an ounce of air was lost nor was a single fissure evidenced in the see-through wheel. Very cool stuff indeed.

A two-sided drive system spins the massive 360-millimeter wheel and tire. The shaft that usually drives the rear sprocket was teamed with a jackshaft that sends power to the opposite side of the wheel, dividing the power equally to both drive chains. The rear brake disc, purloined from a go-cart, also is mounted to this shaft and helps a bit in slowing the long chassis to a halt.

This one-of-a-kind transfer case delivers power through a series of perfectly meshed gears. Heaven help the wayward sparrow that flies too close.

The power source is a 113-cubic-inch Patrick motor massaged by Road-Hawgs. The polished motor is fitted with a set of transparent head covers accented with red. A Davinci carb snakes to the motor's left side with a long-necked intake, and a pair of upturned exhaust tubes faces north on the right. The exhaust is a Road-Hawgs part that looks great and delivers enough decibels to wake the dead.

A Baker five-speed gearbox runs with a BDL clutch and Road-Hawgs primary. This is no ordinary primary that uses a belt to transfer power. A mechanical set of gears mesh with one another as they pass the power from end to end. The open layout exposes the gears for inspection, but begs to have a bit of debris make its way into the mechanism's teeth. The setup runs with little noise, but does sound a bit like a supercharger at full chat, which is music to the ears. The front-mounted oil cooler was created from the transparent element used elsewhere, and the shape is another throwback to Jerry's old-school thinking. Making up for the paltry rear disc brake, the front wheel is grafted with a pair of large-diameter Vendetta rotors from Metal Monsters. Each of these drilled discs is slowed by a six-piston caliper, reducing speed quickly and confidently.

The fuel tank thrusts upward and carries a chrome ornament atop its deeply curved contours.

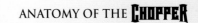

Compared with the long list of radical and unique features on Clear and Present Danger, the rest of the parts list seems to pale a bit. A set of bars from Road-Hawgs sits at the end of the Eurocomponents risers. Grooved, metal grips from Chips were modified by Road-Hawgs, and Paul Yaffe mirrors show you what's growing smaller in a hurry.

Considering the intense level of never-before-seen hardware and an amazing attention to detail, it's a wonder that only three months were required to build Clear and Present Danger. Jerry's history and reputation will more than likely lead to some future creations, and we can't wait to see what's next.

EXILE CYCLES

As a self-proclaimed "bastard child of the motorcycle industry," Exile Cycles owner Russell Mitchell makes no bones about his products or services. Exile has a catalog full of choppers that defy the typical definition of the word, and Russell is proud of it. According to Exile's Web site, one of its goals is to sell "clean, tough European styling" to American buyers and avoid "fancy, frivolous and ridiculous" machines. No one says those other machines are wrong, but Russell will have no part of that market.

Lacking flashy paint, high-gloss finishes and chrome, Exile Cycles choppers have a distinct look in a world full of bright colors and exuberant creations. None of Exile's machines is dull, and Russell makes no excuses for their cost either. A complete, ready-to-ride cycle runs anywhere from $25,000 to way above $40,000, depending on how you want it equipped. A wide variety of chassis, motors and trim await the Exile buyer, so the odds of building two bikes the same are somewhere between slim and none. Names like Bullfighter, Steamroller, Mad Max

Chop, and Fat-Tracker can all be found on Exile Cycles' Web site, each offering another angle on the low-flash theme. Noted buyers of late include actor George Clooney and musician Chris Cornell, the front man for supergroups Audioslave and Soundgarden.

Exile also offers a huge catalog of individual components for those wanting to upgrade their own scoots or build one from the ground up. Exile fills another niche as the exclusive North American importer of SJP Engineering products from Holland. Along with his renowned bike-building prowess, Russell has a notable presence on television through his Build or Bust program on the Discovery Channel. Of course, he also has participated in the Discovery Channel's Biker Build-Off series, providing additional exposure of his talent and personality.

Whether you choose to have Exile Cycles build your dream chopper or merely use it as a source for your own high-end creation, don't mention chrome, glittering paint or flashy accessories. That's not what Russell Mitchell is all about, and he'll be the first to tell you.

Russell Mitchell

BROWN PEARL

Exile Cycles

n arranging to photograph a few of Exile Cycles' machines for this book, I left the selection process up to Exile owner Russell Mitchell and his crew. I knew everything he built was an amazing statement of talent in a slightly different package. When Russell himself rolled up to the studio I had assembled in Daytona Beach, Fla., aboard Brown Pearl, I was thrown for a loop. Although not expecting chrome and glossy paint, I wasn't prepared for a machine that looked like it had spent the last 30 years under water.

Upon closer examination and by reading the stats provided, I learned the premature aging process was born from the Discovery Channel's *Build or Bust* series and was exclusive to Exile Cycles. I discovered it takes more work to create the look on Brown Pearl than it does to apply the more traditional paint and chrome add-ons. I know Russell doesn't cut corners when building a chopper, so the resulting machine is unpolished by design.

An Exile Cycles rigid chassis riding on a 40-degree rake and a 2-inch stretch in the down tubes is the basis for the build. Adding another 6 degrees of rake in the SJP Engineering triple trees throws the SJP Tech Glide forks way out in front. The fork legs also were lengthened 6 inches for the final, aggressive geometry.

A Total Performance motor displaces 121 cubic inches and provides tire-smoking power on demand. A Super G carburetor from S&S feeds the beast, and a Crane HI-4 ignition provides the fire. A set of Exile Monster Shotgun pipes leads the exiting gases away without hesitation. The short tubes do nothing to quell the noise pounding from the motor, but what's power without a little racket?

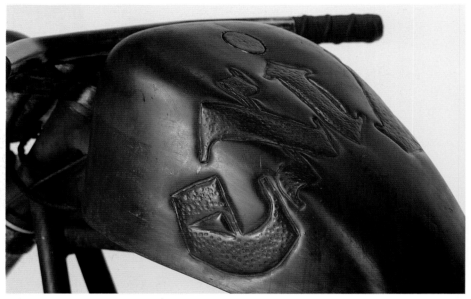

The blacksmith fuel tank was prematurely aged. "Exile" was hand chiseled into the sheet metal for some added flair.

A pair of low-slung drag bars sits astride the Exile risers and conceals the throttle cables. It features grips wrapped with hockey tape.

Fork legs, wheel rims, spokes, and brake components were aged by applying a corrosive acid wash and then removing it after a certain time.

Monster Shotgun exhaust pipes show spent fumes the exit with a minimum of fuss and noise suppression.

The six-speed gearbox is a Jim's product combined with a Rivera clutch and Primo primary. Shifting between gears is achieved by depressing the foot clutch, grabbing the truncated suicide lever, and slipping into the next ratio in line. The innovative line-lock allows the rider to hold the brakes in an "on" position, thus freeing one of his boots to hold the bike upright when stopped, especially on a hill. It's subtle yet ingenious.

Brown Pearl's ancient appearance was achieved through a variety of means. The blacksmith fuel tank carries the Exile logo, hammered into place by a skilled hand. The tank's sheet metal, as well as the rest of the machine, was aged with a proprietary corrosive acid that is applied and then removed, resulting in the left-in-the-barn look. Every inch of steel was treated with

this process, thus providing a consistently rugged appearance.

Additional spills can be found on the 15-inch Exile oil bag and short Trojan 10 1/2-inch rear fender. Even the spokes of the Monster Wheel rims were aged in compliance with the theme. A fairly moderate 230-series tire out back fits Exile's attitude, but goes against the current trend of 300-millimeter and larger tires. Since going against the grain is part of Russell Mitchell's approach, this suits him fine.

Exile braking components provide more than ample slowing power on Brown Pearl. Discs at both ends are squeezed by multiple-piston calipers. The front carries a four-piston; a pair out back grabs the Exile sprocket-rotor unit. With twist controls on both ends of the Exile bars, you'll find

Exile Cycles has mastered the art of combining the drive sprocket and brake disc into a single unit. Brown Pearl uses a prematurely aged example.

Measuring 121 cubic inches in displacement, the Total Performance motor only looks like it's lived its life in a barn, but it delivers modern power at the twist of the throttle.

none of the usual hand levers here. The foot pegs, foot-clutch lever and handgrips were wrapped with hockey tape to complete the vintage appearance. An Exile seat pan was wrapped in natural, aged leather and was stitched with rough-hewn laces around the perimeter by Bill Wall.

Brown Pearl may not be at the top of everyone's chopper shopping list, but Exile Cycles doesn't pander to everyone. It prefers clients who can discern between the ordinary and the not so ordinary, and are willing to pay the price for this exclusivity.

HOT ROD

Exile Cycles

ot Rod has served two purposes for Exile Cycles since its inception. When concocting the theme, the Exile team wanted something that heralded the bygone era of 1950s hot rods. Custom cars built then were straightforward, carried big motors, and almost always sported whitewall tires. The first Exile Hot Rod was for the Discovery Channel's *Biker Build-Off* program. The need to build something fresh for the show and the desire to create a '50s-style machine turned out to be a perfect match. Since the first example was assembled, it has gone on to become one of Exile's most popular models.

As with period customs of the day, this hot rod carries a big 121-cubic-inch motor from Total Performance. Built to be powerful and almost bullet proof, the TP engine line is often the first choice of contemporary chopper builders who demand the best. A set of heat-tape-wrapped Monster Drag pipes from Exile features trumpet tips at the business end of each blacked-out tube. A Jim's six-speed tranny is mounted to a Rivera clutch and Primo transfer.

Total Performance supplied Hot Rod with its 121-cubic-inch mill. A brushed finish is accessorized by satin black trim.

Providing a safe harbor for the motor is a rigid Exile Hot Rod frame. A mild 32-degree angle on the steering head is uncommon in these days of extremely raked machines, but as always, Russell Mitchell likes his bikes to roll in the face of convention. Exile Sani-Trees hold the fork legs in place, with the lower segments taken from a Harley-Davidson FLT. Before installation, the right caliper mount was surgically removed with another inch added to the length, and the legs were powder-coated in the now famous semigloss black we so often see on Russell's creations.

Rolling stock on Hot Rod is another bit of the out of the ordinary,

except when you're dealing with an Exile chopper. The 230-millimeter rear tire wears an Exile whitewall, as does the 200-millimeter front. Having a large tire at both ends enhances handling and provides a luxury-car ride. Red rims are filled with satin chrome spokes, keeping the level of flash to a minimum. Both rims are 15 inches in diameter with a 5-inch-wide hoop up front and a 7-inch on the aft. A single 11 1/2-inch rotor gets grabbed by a four-piston caliper on the leading wheel, and an Exile sprocket-rotor rides out behind. Exile's line-lock system also is installed for braking on an incline.

The line-lock button provides the rider with an extra margin of safety when stopping on a hill and frees up one of his boots to hold the scooter upright.

The King Sportster tank is finished in satin black with silver flames and red stripes, just like a rod from the bygone era.

A 3 1/2-inch halogen light from SJP Engineering in Holland lights the path at night.

Billet pegs and the foot clutch are Exile components and, as with the rest of Hot Rod, are satin finished.

Exile Cycles' well-known drive-sprocket and brake-rotor combo saves weight and complexity.

In its natural state, the leather covering the LePera seat pan makes a perfect statement aboard Hot Rod.

Unlike many of today's more typical choppers, Hot Rod rides on a 200-series front tire to better match the profile of the 230 rear.

The bare-essentials theme continues when we reach the sheet-metal division. A King Sportster tank rides on the top rail and is trimmed in satin black with silver flames. A quick wipe down with WD-40 is all the bodywork needs to keep its cool, including the short Trojan rear fender. The spirit of the '50s hot rod lives on by the absence of a front fender. A 15-inch oil bag from Exile doesn't escape the semigloss motif and is nestled behind the motor's rear cylinder as usual. Blacked-out Highbars feature integral risers for a clean and classic look that melds perfectly with the ongoing ensemble. Leather in its natural state covers the LePera seat pan, with Paul Cox taking credit for the work.

Hot Rod's simplicity doesn't mean it can be cranked out quickly. Depending on requested options, three months may be required before you can take delivery. As we have all been told, good things take time and are worth the wait.

Builder: Wide Open Cycles
Owner: Bobby Clark

Based in Daytona Beach, Fla., Wide Open Cycles gets its fair share of exposure at two major events held there annually. Between Bike Week in March and Biktoberfest in October, nearly a million people make the journey to soak up the sun and see a few hundred thousand custom bikes. It takes something amazing to stand out from the rest in this sea of chrome and lacquer. As it is ridden down Main Street, or any other street, Sexy draws more than its share of stares and is only one example of what the Daytona builder can do.

An Independence Low Life chassis provides the build's low and sleek demeanor. With 4 inches up and 7 inches out added to the 46-degree rake, an even stealthier profile is attained. Controlling the chassis on the road is an American Suspension fork from the Phantom series. Another 4-inch over was thrown in the composition for more attitude. Legend Air allows the rider to adjust his ride height and responds with the touch of a button. Not everyone thinks riding a chopper should be painful.

When a chopper is this good looking, you don't require an enormous motor to do your bidding. Still, Wide Open didn't want to sacrifice performance, so an S&S 96-cubic-inch V-twin was combined with a Prowler six-speed gearbox. A Baker clutch delivers a smooth transition as the power is sent through the Primo Brute IV primary. Final drive consists of a nickel-plated chain that rotates a K-Tec sprocket. A pair of L.A.F. exhaust pipes slithers from the mounting points to become conjoined twins before allowing a raucous exit.

A set of Wide Open Cycles handlebars, with hidden cables and non-existent risers, keeps the overall design clean.

The bike isn't named "Sexy" for nothing, and the tiny pole dancer helps secure the moniker in chrome.

Formed completely from scratch, the fuel tank on Sexy is just that.

The left side of the Florida Kustom rear hoop is wide open
because the sprocket and rotor combination is mounted on the opposite side.

Wide Open handcrafted the flowing bodywork, which appears as if it were shaved from a single billet of aluminum. Snuggled beneath the luxurious form is an Independent Cycle oil tank, which keeps the lubricant safe and discreetly located. Slung into the panels' midriff is a saddle created by Wide Open Cycles and upholstered with help from Daytona Upholstery. The sculpted handlebars, custom made by Wide Open, are devoid of risers.

Adding to the build's sterile nature are throttle and brake cables mounted internally, thus avoiding common clutter. Comfort Controls provided the grips and control levers, which are required even with the lack of external piping. An Arlen Ness mirror provides a clear view to the rear.

Metzeler ME880 rubber at both ends keeps the Florida Kustom wheels on the straight and narrow, even though the rear rubber is anything but. Perhaps not as wild as the 360-millimeter monsters, a 280 provides an ample footprint while retaining a svelte contour for the rear sheet metal. The front brake rotor is another Florida Kustom component; its progress is halted by an American Suspension caliper. A K-Tec Eurocomponent sprotor handles the drive and stopping duties on the rear hoop.

Sexy was built for the Strip Tease Clothing Co. Strip Tease raffled the bike for Animal Resource Network Inc., which is devoted to rescuing animals from being destroyed by finding them quality homes. The raffle brought in more than $52,000 and certainly spared the lives of a few lovable pets. In this case, being Sexy also means having a heart.

PARAGON

Wide Open Cycles
Lynn Jones Custom Works

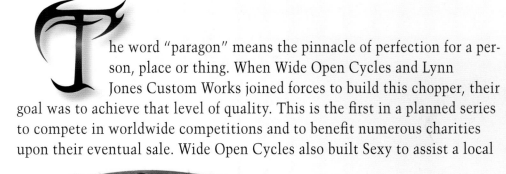

he word "paragon" means the pinnacle of perfection for a person, place or thing. When Wide Open Cycles and Lynn Jones Custom Works joined forces to build this chopper, their goal was to achieve that level of quality. This is the first in a planned series to compete in worldwide competitions and to benefit numerous charities upon their eventual sale. Wide Open Cycles also built Sexy to assist a local

charity, bringing some good press into the sometimes dark world of motorcycles. Facing the challenge of creating a bike the likes of which have never been seen, Lynn Jones and Wide Open sharpened their pencils and hit the ground running.

Chosen for Paragon's core was a chassis from Penz Performance, and the dimensions set the tone for the rest of the build. A steep 52-degree rake is embelished by another 10 inches up, 22 inches over and 10 inches out. Add to these numbers an RC Components Wide Glide fork extended by 22 inches and you begin to picture Paragon's tall, radical

stance. Wanting to build a chopper that was as comfortable to ride as it was appealing to look at, the builders included a rear suspension on the spec sheet. It is comprised of a Penz Performance swing arm and Legends Air shocks. RC Components triple trees hold a set of Wide Open Cycles handlebars hostage with Custom Cycle Controls grips and hand levers. The bar design eliminates the need for risers, adding to Paragon's uncluttered look.

The frame tubes, fuel tank and rear fender were blended so masterfully that it's hard to discern where one ends and the next begins. The

A chin fairing includes frenched driving lights in keeping with the sculpted theme of the Paragon.

Not a spot on Paragon is left without some artistic blending of metal, and the forks are no exception.

fuel tank was formed from scratch by the talented crew at Wide Open and trail back in one motion to reach the ostrich-covered saddle. At the bottom of the frame's down tubes we find a sculpted bit of pointed art in the chin spoiler. The Penz Performance Soft Tail oil tank was artfully concealed beneath the section of bodywork that falls beneath the saddle, which also keeps the rear suspension components hidden from view. Stainless-steel lines keep the flow smooth and the appearance sterile.

The front fender is another handmade bit from Wide Open and is molded into the lower fork legs, again delivering a seamless application of several items. As with the rest of the sheet metal, the front and rear fenders were created exclusively for Paragon, adding value to the bottom line. Stainless-steel foot controls and pegs also were styled and manufactured for Paragon, growing the list of handmade items to unheard of levels.

RC Components Bandit wheels and front brake rotor may have been catalog items, but fit right in with this bike's custom nature. Avon

Carrying only 88 inches of displacement, Paragon is still a powerful ride due largely to the turbocharger mounted to the V-twin motor.

Venom tires were stretched over both rims, with a 250-millimeter for traction. It's driven by a pulley and brake-rotor unit by RC. Four-piston calipers were mounted to both braking surfaces for sure and certain stopping.

Paragon's engine bay is no less interesting, although a bit more off-the-shelf stuff was used to build the motor. The 88-cubic-inch Harley-Davidson motor was largely untouched internally. Pedestrian items like spark plugs and wires also are hidden from view, and a remote starter can bring the bike to life from a distance. An S&S Model G carburetor breathes through an RC Components Air Forced 1 air cleaner for utility and great

looks. Once the air flows through the cleaner and carb, things get moving quickly as the turbocharger spins up and rams the oxygen into the motor with intensity. A puffer compensates easily for any lack of big-inch displacement. Any stray gases remaining make a speedy exit through the Turbo exhaust from RC Components. The factory five-speed gearbox ships the power to the drive pulley through a Primo clutch and primary. A Gates belt keeps things quiet and clean.

Paragon's sale will benefit cancer research and art and literacy programs for children. As fans of custom choppers, we earn the benefit of being able to enjoy the artwork that is Paragon.

EL REY

Warren Lane (The Neighborhood King)

Warren Lane may not be as well known as his brother Billy, but we're sure to see more of him in coming years if he continues to build bikes like El Rey. Vast exposure in motorcycle media has boosted his visibility, but the quality of his designs and craftsmanship will carry him far into the future.

The definition of a "chopper" defies concrete boundaries. Yes, many cycles wear elongated front forks and ride on impossibly bizarre frames, but Warren chose a more traditional path for El Rey. Construction began with a 1957 Harley-Davidson frame with no modifications to the dimensions, save a 1-inch stretch to the top tube behind the seat. Although the frame's dimensions were changed little, the steel tubes were replaced mostly by twisted lengths of stainless steel. The steering head and bottom and vertical seat tubes were the only ones not replaced with stainless-steel sections. The resulting combination is unique. Another bit of Harley-Davidson hardware is found on the front forks, which were taken from a 1934 VLD. Warren modified the assembly's front legs to meet his own design parameters.

Extensive use of stainless segments can be found on nearly every corner of the bike.

El Rey was conceived with a true old-school look in mind, but when it came to choosing a power plant, contemporary mechanics were selected. A pair of S&S cylinders is mounted on the Delkron cases and filled with S&S pistons and connecting rods. The 93-cubic-inch displacement means El Rey is no slouch when it hits the streets of Miami or anywhere else. STD heads, Sifton cams and a set of valves from Rowe make up the motor's internals and related equipment. A Morris magneto delivers the spark, and a pair of Warren Lane pipes, wrapped in retro heat tape, provides a swift egress for departing fumes. The horsepower is fed into a six-speed gearbox via the BDL clutch and Warren Lane primary. Red links on the drive chain add another hint of color to the mostly silver and black chopper.

The largely hand-built fuel tank is finished with a softly burnished patina and a classic set of pinstripes.

Stainless steel twisted into an art form carries most of El Rey's components. The polished finish adds some dazzle to the overall appearance.

Warren Lane also crafted a set of Oakland-style handlebars for his retro bobber.

Part of El Rey's allure comes from the 23-inch, semiknobby front tire teamed with an 18-inch hoop on the back end. Not wanting to disobey all of the old-school rules, Warren used a mild 240-millimeter for the rear rubber. He laced up the spoke rims before installing the rolling stock onto the bike. The front hub lacks brake hardware, and an Exile Cycles sprocket-rotor and caliper are responsible for all required hauling down from speed. Both wheels are trimmed with a custom-machined piece at their centers; it features a multistepped cone with three-pointed spinners.

Except for the modified West Coast Choppers fuel tank, Warren hand formed all of El Rey's sheet metal. That includes the rear fender,

oil tank, handlebars, and grips. Even the foot pegs and levers are from Warren's mind and were cut for this machine only. A 1941 Willys headlight sheds some wattage up front, and a 1954 Cessna donated the rear stoplight.

It took a year to create El Rey, and the high level of detail shows where the time went. The mostly silver leaf paint is highlighted by black, red and white accents, and just the right amount of period-correct pinstriping. Even lifting the small saddle shows the steel panel beneath was trimmed to match what's visible on top. Warren also crafted the seat, showing that his abilities have no limit.

SCREW THIS

Redneck Engineering

edneck Engineering has a simple mission: build "really cool, functional and affordable motorcycles for everyday folks." With that outlook, you might expect Redneck's cycles and related parts to lack quality or creativity, but you'd be dead wrong. Although Redneck's prices are not as high as some others, the builder's imagination and quality are surprisingly high.

Screw This was built for the 2005 Heritage Motorcycle Rally Bike Build-Off. Redneck Engineering was among 10 selected builders competing for the $100,000 prize. Among the glittering and flashy bikes at the event, Screw This seemed a bit dowdy at first glance but became a crowd favorite before the week-long deal was over. Attention to detail and unusual use of finishes raised the bike to new heights. Although not the winner of the top prize, it scored well with the public and judges alike.

Built from Redneck's Curves chassis, Screw This carries some fairly radical geometry. A rake of 48 degrees has another 6 inches out and 4 inches up thrown into the package. A lengthy, tubular springer front fork, another Redneck Engineering product, sits way out in front of the

rider, adding to the chopper's radical nature. Coated in glossy black to match the frame tubes, the fork was fitted with chrome springs to do the dirty work. The ultrasleek fuel tank was crafted for the build-off and is the only example in existence. The tank's elongated curvature reaches from the steering head all the way back to the saddle with an exaggerated and muscular contour. To keep the bike's design clean and uncluttered, there is no oil tank. The required fluids are carried in the frame tubes.

The simple lines of Screw This are the result of an amalgam of high-tech trickery that defies its outward appearance. Redneck's talented staff is responsible for the bending, shaping, welding, and installation of every facet of

Holding the fuel is the Hot Rod tank, a one-of-a-kind piece from Redneck. It may not hold much gas, but it does a great job at holding your attention.

the bike's sheet metal and chassis, proving their worth as world-class builders, despite their simple approach. The rear fender, such as it is, was hand-rolled from flat sheet metal and features tubular edging for another contoured detail. As mentioned earlier, the design's visual simplicity is quickly overwhelmed by a raft of amazing details. Common fittings – such as foot pegs, handgrips and control levers – are also Redneck Engineering bits, thus trimming the list of outside sources required to complete the project.

Although highly capable, the Redneck staff leaned on vendors for certain components, including the Weld Racing wheels. They were purchased off the shelf, but Redneck gave some attention to the rims before installation. The perforated, five-spoke design is finished in a tasteful

combination of satin silver and wrinkle black, keeping the flash to a minimum while adding another facet to the overall theme. Both brake rotors hail from Redneck as well but are grabbed by an HHI caliper on the fore rim and an Exile unit on the aft. Another bit of Redneck genius is the one-pedal braking system. Instead of cluttering the bike with a brake pedal and a front brake lever, both brakes are employed by stepping on the solo pedal. This balanced system sends the right amount of squeeze to each end, stopping Screw This safely and confidently every time.

The thinly padded excuse for a saddle also resulted from Redneck teaming up with an outside source. Outlaw Customs provided the basic shell for the seat, then upholstered the component in Caiman after

A 97-cubic-inch V-twin from Accurate Engineering powers Screw This briskly and looks great doing it.

A set of Squished exhaust comes from Redneck Engineering. It is fitted with satin chrome heat shields and exit tips.

At the top end of the Redneck tubular fork is the set of springs responsible for putting some motion into the chassis.

Redneck turned its attention to the details. Rear suspension is limited to whatever cushion the piston attached to the bottom of the pillion can provide.

Another set of outside components was used to assemble the V-twin mill that powers Screw This. An Accurate Engineering 97-cubic-inch motor includes STD heads and an S&S Model G carburetor. The motor replicates an early Harley Panhead and is finished mostly in the same satin silver found on the wheels for continuity. Air inlets and exhaust are Redneck parts; the exit tubes are Squished models. The matte-black pipes are accented by a pair of tapered, chrome shields for looks and a bit of insulation from the heat. A Roadmax six-speed gearbox is mated to the clutch and transfer, which hail from BDL. The red-sided final drive chain is a CCI product and adds just the right touch of color to a pedestrian item.

A classic black includes a set of yellow, red and orange flames, all done in House of Kolor hues. The shapes, paint and details create a unique machine, and that's just what Redneck Engineering had in mind. Interested in buying Screw This? Take a number and wait your turn.

MAD ATLAS

Mad Wrench Custom Cycles

As the proprietor of Mad Wrench Custom Cycles, Brad Ruel has seen his machines grace the pages of numerous books and magazines. Not one to rest on his laurels and build the same bike over and over, Ruel has a style that is all over the map. On Mad Atlas, the map is all over the bike. Built in conjunction with *Biker's Atlas* publisher Scott Goodnight, Mad Atlas has paint and trim depicting a large U.S. map, complete with biker destinations.

The 114-cubic-inch V-twin came from Mid-USA and was polished to a high shine.

Beginning with a Heavy Hitter frame from Mad Wrench's catalog, the radical geometry was altered to excessive dimensions. Another 14 inches over and 6 inches out are joined by a stretch of 8 inches. The normal rake of 45 degrees is a moot point when altering the rest of the numbers in this fashion. The single-down-tube layout delivers looks and performance. Adding to the chassis' craziness is the Phantom inverted fork from American Suspension. The tubes also were bolstered by another 14 inches, and the upper legs are finished in black powder coat. Mad Wrench Custom Cycles modified the forks with an American Suspension integrated brake caliper and hid the brake lines from view. These tricks get bikes published.

A set of smooth-top triple trees hold the steering tubes in place and feature handlebars that also hail from The Wrench. Rear suspension is a combination of a Spear swing arm from The Wrench and Legends Air Ride shocks. The angular and sensuous fuel tank hosts the bulk of the map graphics. Stainless Creations crafted the design. The form reaches back to embrace the chassis' upper segment and keeps rolling in one consistent movement. The Wrench was responsible for the 4-quart oil tank that rides below the solo saddle.

Russ Wernimont created both fenders to hug the tires with little room for error. Pearl Tangerine paint forms the base for the highly detailed

Adding to the bike's detail, each of the Ego Tripp wheel spokes features a compass direction.

The *Biker's Atlas* logo was emblazoned on the primary and highlights the motor's cleanly polished look.

Created in conjunction with *Biker's Atlas* publisher Scott Goodnight, the bike's theme is carried onto the 4-quart oil tank and related bodywork.

graphics. The maps and biker hangouts were expertly airbrushed onto the metal. Riding below the sheet-metal shields are wheels from Ego Tripp, which were made for Mad Atlas specifically. Avon rubber was applied to both hoops. The rear donut measures 300 millimeters across. The integrated front caliper seizes the sides of an Ego Tripp rotor upon demand; rear brakes are from 3 Guys Customs.

Mid-USA delivered the 114-cubic-inch motor, and a Mikuni 45-millimeter carburetor breathes deeply through a Wimmer air cleaner. A set of chrome exhaust tubes sweeps downward before taking a sharp bend north to its exits. These handmade items are another bit of magic from Stainless Creations. A Tauer Machine clutch and primary join the Baker six-speed transmission.

It required four months to create Mad Atlas, but it would take much longer to visit all the places illustrated on its flanks. Makes you want to hit the open road and give it a try.

BAD ATLAS

Mad Wrench Custom Cycles

Bad Atlas was built for Scott Goodnight, publisher of the *Biker's Atlas*. His books detail hundreds of places to go on two wheels – not just sights to see, but restaurants and other businesses that welcome bikers. Bad Atlas wears a more traditional paint scheme than Mad Atlas, but combines a wide variety of hardware and tricks of the trade.

A Phat Daddy frame from Brad Ruel's Mad Wrench Custom Cycles started the build. The rigid chassis rolls with a 42-degree rake joined by 6 inches over, 2 inches out and a stretch of 4 inches. It's not the wildest we've seen, but it can be ridden daily without worry. Control comes from the American Suspension inverted forks, which were lengthened 6 inches.

A large Maltese-cross headlight hails from Russ Wernimont's shop and begins Bad Atlas' overall motif.

Another of Bad Atlas' many Maltese crosses is found on the Karata transfer case.

The requisite skull and crossbones reside on Bad Atlas' tank and carry the bike's name as well.

One hundred spokes fill the holes of the copper-finished rims. The fenders are more Russ Wernimont items.

One of Bad Wrench's hallmarks is the extensive use of a Maltese cross. The first application of this classic shape is found at the headlight, a product of Russ Wernimont. The chrome bezel and lens were cut into the cross' profile and make a nice addition to the theme. Russ also is to thank for the front and rear fenders, which show his range of talent. The remaining sheet metal in the fuel and oil tanks is from The Wrench, illustrating Brad Ruel's talent in three dimensions. The Phat Daddy oil bag holds 6 quarts of precious lubricant, although the all-black finish masks its true dimensions.

Perhaps not as graphically detailed as Mad Atlas, this version claims a bigger motor. The S&S 124-cubic-inch monster is wrapped in polished and chromed hardware. It draws breath through a Wimmer Machine air cleaner and blows out through a large-diameter Wrath exhaust from Stainless Creations. The two-into-one design features an enormous exit orifice that offers no resistance to gases or sound. A clutch and primary from Karata are on duty to handle whichever of the six speeds is chosen by rowing through the Baker gearbox. A Maltese cross, trimmed in copper, appears again on the primary case.

The S&S motor displaces 124 cubic inches and moves Bad Atlas swiftly to any of its chosen locations.

The rigid Phat Daddy chassis carries no rear suspension, but is nicely detailed with a "Bad Atlas" plaque covering the axle mount.

House of Kolor Black and Tangerine paint covers the sheet metal. The rims, which were treated to a copper finish before getting their 100 spokes inserted, carry the motif further. Hallcraft provided the hoops; Avon Super Venom rubber delivers the traction. HHI rotors are slowed by Hallcraft calipers on both wheels for safe and secure stopping.

The saddle was upholstered in a combination of black leather and tan ostrich, and was completed with another Maltese cross.

Four months and the assistance of a variety of industry legends helped bring Bad Atlas to life. They hope the appealing package will bring awareness of motorcycle riding to the public forefront.

INDUSTRIAL DISEASE

Kevin Verkest (Fabricator Kevin Steel Chopper Parts)

Having an extensive background in engineering and fabrication, Kevin Verkest wanted to build something different from today's big-tired, overweight choppers. He set out to build a bobber to "hot rod around on." He achieved his goal by combining a variety of vintage techniques with current technology. With help from a few industry heavy hitters, the result is an amazing bike that almost defies description, except for perhaps "cool."

Holding the oil in check is a Fabricator Kevin tank complete with pressure gauge. The brass-knuckle kick-start pedal is another nice touch. ▶

Wanting to keep the bike close to old school, Kevin chose a rigid frame from Paughco to begin the project. The 30-degree rake ensures crisp handling. No other frame dimensions were altered. Kevin didn't mess with the geometry but did remove any factory mounting lugs before continuing production. Kevin's goal was to build a bike that handled as well as it accelerated, so a set of 35-millimeter Harley-Davidson Superglide forks were shortened by 2 inches before being slid into the Sifton triple trees. This approach kept the wheelbase short and the geometry more like a sport bike than a chopper.

Harley-Davidson also was tapped for the engine – an 80-cubic-inch Shovelhead built by Dan Roedel. K&B slugs ride in the Harley cylinders, and Sifton bump sticks tell the valves when to move and how fast. Maintaining the bike's simplicity, a Keihin CV carburetor was attached, with air filtered by a Goodson cleaner. A Morris MM-74 magneto continues the vintage theme and looks like something borrowed from a full-blown drag bike.

A Mustang tank from Paughco holds the fossil fuel in place and is decorated with the bike's name.

Going right to the source of all things V-twin, Kevin installed an 80-cubic-inch Shovelhead motor from Harley in Industrial Disease.

More items that remind us of a quarter-mile machine are the truncated exhaust pipes that snake from one side of the motor to the other and end abruptly after turning south. With nothing to suppress the sound, a cacophony of noise is expelled from their orifices. No one said old school was quiet. A four-speed gearbox from a 1979 Harley-Davidson FLH stands ready for duty and uses a Barnett clutch and Karata primary to send the motivation to the Fabricator Kevin rear sprocket. There are no belts or shaft drives here, only a simple real-world chain.

With a caliper from a Suzuki GSXR 750 grabbing a 10-inch Russell rotor, Industrial Disease has swift and sure braking.

A set of original pipes leads the fumes away from the motor but does nothing to quiet the roar that emanates from within.

To keep things from dragging on the pavement, Kevin installed a Superglide front rim wrapped with a Metzeler ME880 tire between the front forks. The rear wheel is actually a 15-inch automotive rim from Weld Racing, again mated to an ME880 donut. Tokico brake calipers borrowed from two Suzukis cease the motion upon demand by holding the Russell 10-inch rotors. This mix of old and new is mounted

to the machine by specially fabricated brackets courtesy of Fabricator Kevin.

Sheet metal is another mixed bag with items coming from across the globe. A Paughco Mustang fuel tank is stopped up by a gas cap taken from a 1971 Honda 350. Kevin fabbed the oil bag from stainless steel and added an all-important oil gauge to monitor the temperature of the fluid within. Eric Gorges from Voodoo Choppers lent a hand in bending the tire-hugging rear fender. No self-respecting bobber owner would even think of using a front fender, so Industrial Disease rolls without one.

Continuing the theme of not using the same vendor too often, Kevin included a headlight from Bates, a taillight of his own creation, and handlebars by Chrome Werks, held in place by Sifton risers. Harley-Davidson provided the grips, foot pegs and controls, and JayBrake was enlisted for the hand levers. Goblin Millworx supplied the Asphalt Pic mirrors, and the seat was born of LePera. The final touch was a hand-blown glass shift knob produced by Shamrock Fabrication. Omaha Orange is the scoot's primary hue, with a black tank band heralding the bike's moniker. Tasteful pinstriping on the frame and sheet metal completes the package.

It took Kevin only six months to assemble Industrial Disease, and his blend of old and new is truly remarkable.

CUSTOM SHOP CYCLES

Flanagan, Ill., with a population hovering around 1,000, is hardly a teeming metropolis, but Custom Shop Cycles has called it home for well over a decade. John Wargo runs the shop and has been building custom cars and cycles since he was 15. His first endeavor was a 1975 Firebird, which he bought and then customized. After his handy work won a few awards, he realized others might want him to do the same for their vehicles. His first two-wheeled ride was a Honda CB400, which he bought when he was 18. Having expanded his craft to two-wheeled vehicles, John found that he enjoyed the work and was always getting requests to do something new.

Most of his early work involved painting cars with any number of custom colors and designs, and that led to the assembly of motorcycles. Once this hurdle was jumped, it was only a short step to creating choppers from the ground up. Custom Shop Cycles has built close to 30 choppers for customers and earned numerous awards. Starting with a clean slate, Custom Shop Cycles can build a bike costing $15,000 to $150,000 depending on the owner's tastes and budget. Those are the only parameters keeping John in line, and since he is capable of welding, bodywork, painting, and air brushing, there's no stopping his creative freight train once it gets rolling.

PURPLE GATOR

Custom Shop Cycles

B uilt for an employee of Custom Shop Cycles, Purple Gator was conceived as a radical bike that would retain a "classy and clean" appearance. That wasn't an easy goal, but John and his crew were worthy of the challenge.

Starting with a rigid chassis from Accessories Unlimited, the team brought some exclusivity to the catalog frame. Three inches were added to the backbone, and another 6 inches up were thrown into the mix. The 45-degree rake was mated to another 7 degrees in the Spike triple trees. Desiring a clean chopper, Custom Shop integrated the fuel pump into the

frame's down tube. The inverted front forks also are from Spike and feature a 14-inch stretch, adding to this creation's radical nature.

No chopper worth its salt carries a weenie motor in the frame, so a 127-cubic-inch Ultima mill powers Purple Gator briskly. Bringing much needed air into the V-twin is a set of Weber velocity stacks mated to a carburetor of the same make. A 45-degree intake leads the blend of fuel and air into the cylinders, where the Accel Dual Fire ignition delivers the spark. Any remaining gases are shown the door through a set of Hooker straight-cut pipes.

An Accessories Unlimited six-speed gearbox ships the selected ratio through a Barnett clutch and BDL primary before reaching the GMA pulley and brake system.

Of course, all the horsepower in the world means little unless it's joined by equally impressive sheet metal, and as we have learned, John Wargo's team was up to the task. Custom Shop fabricated the fuel receptacle, which draws back cleanly to the rider's pillion. A modified oil bag from Accessories Unlimited joins the fray. An Arlen Ness front and Milwaukee Iron rear fender complete the bike's metal needs.

Handmade by John Wargo, the fuel tank glides back smoothly to reach the saddle.

An open-belt primary rides below the Ultima motor's painted cylinders.

Custom Chrome handlebars feature risers that are part of the assembly, making for a cleaner appearance.

◄ Weber carbs tower over the fuel tank and breathe in through chrome velocity stacks.

Straight-cut exhaust pipes make for easy breathing.

The Custom Chrome handlebars, finished off with Hurst brake and clutch levers, are devoid of risers. Hurst also supplied the foot pegs and controls for a consistent look. Before using any of the controls, the rider settles his haunches onto the Corbin Alligator Pearl saddle. The Weld Racing EVO Tri-Bar rims are wrapped with Avon Venom rubber out back and a Metzeler ME880 skin up front. Front anchors come in the form of a Weld Racing EVO Tri-Bar rotor, which is snagged by an HHI four-piston caliper. GMA provided the pulley and brake-rotor package out back along with four-piston calipers.

An alligator effect augmented the Purple Kandy paint from PPG. John is to blame for the impeccable finish. Only 30 days were needed to get Purple Gator on the road, showing that Custom Shop Cycles is fast and amazing at building custom choppers.

HOOKED UP

Custom Shop Cycles

Hooked Up represents the chopper segment in a trio of machines built for the Hooker Headers company. A Dodge truck and a full-dresser cycle completed the triangle, and all were finished in similar wardrobe. The vehicles' show tour brought a new level of attention to Hooker and Custom Shop Cycles.

Wally World Custom Choppers provided the Stingray Soft Tail chassis. With suspension at both ends, Hooked Up would be as comfortable to ride as it is cool to look at. One inch over, 3 inches out and a stretch of 1 inch were added to the 48-degree rake for a usable geometry, which proves a show bike can be ridden hard on the street. Frame modifications included the saddle's low-slung, drop-seat position and oil storage in the frame, thus eliminating the need for a separate tank.

Another foot was added to the Fat Street forks from Mean Street. Fat Street triple trees also were employed, carrying another 5 degrees of rake as well as custom-built handlebars. Hanging beneath the lower triple tree is the first of three Lazer Star headlights. These tiny yet powerful lamps throw a tightly focused beam of light onto the road ahead. Another pair of lamps is mounted to the lower section of the frame's down tube. Rear shocks from Progressive provide the comfort and travel for the rear swing arm.

A variety of sources was tapped for the bike's sheet metal, starting with a Custom Shop Cycles 4-gallon peanut fuel tank. Typically, a peanut tank holds only 2 gallons, but John wanted Hooked Up to be able to run longer between fill-ups. Front and rear fender metal came from Milwaukee Iron, and the rear was shortened. To maintain consistency, Hurst again supplied the grips, hand levers, foot pegs, and controls. Tooled ostrich leather covers the Corbin saddle, and DuPont Candy Blue and Yellow Pearl paint was applied to the bodywork. The tribal flames set off the yellow hue and flow smoothly toward the chopper's rear.

Twin carburetors from Weber feed the basic fuel and air mixture into the twin cylinders.

Casting their light from the lower down tube, the Lazer Star units set the night ablaze.

Feeling a bit down on your luck? Maybe a boost from the nitrous-oxide system will put a smile on your wind-stretched face.

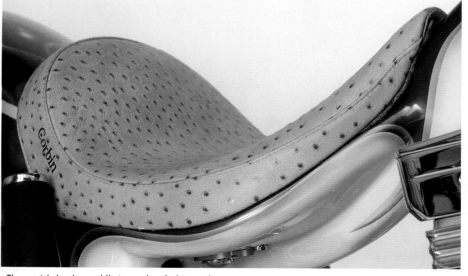

The ostrich-leather saddle is another Corbin product.

The Total Performance motor displaces 121 cubic inches and is fed by a multitude of fluids. ▶

A 4-gallon peanut tank from Custom Cycle Shop rests just behind the drag-style bars and digital instrument cluster.

The alloy rims were designed by Custom Shop Cycles and then machined to life by Ego Tripp. The matching set was made exclusively for Hooked Up. A 300-millimeter expanse of Venom rear rubber from Avon rolls with a sister donut of 120 millimeters up front. Both brake rotors also were custom machined by Ego Tripp after being drawn by Custom Shop Cycles. HHI calipers carry six pistons in the front and another four in the rear. More than adequate braking power is on tap, matching the horsepower delivered by the Total Performance motor.

Measuring 121 cubic inches in displacement, the TP lump is fitted with a pair of Weber carburetors, each one sprouting from a side of the motor. Accel ignition fires the mess to life whether or not the nitrous-oxide button is depressed. Upon demand, the added juice of the NOS pushes Hooked Up into warp speed with little fuss. Because it's a Hooker corporate bike, it stands to reason the exhaust would hail from the company's own catalog. Short Slash is the model. Baker delivered the six-speed gearbox and primary, and a Barnett clutch provides the required slip between gears.

Standing alone on a company's turntable, Hooked Up would draw a fair amount of attention. Combined with the bagger and Dodge truck, the results must have been staggering.

POINTLESS

Tempest Cycles Inc.

With an extensive background in assembling high-end choppers, Tempest Cycles Inc. was an obvious choice to be one of 10 builders selected to enter the 2005 Heritage Motorcycle Rally Bike Build-Off in Charleston, S.C. Tempest's gifted staff has a blend of abilities that allows it to produce choppers from high-quality components, many of which are created from scratch.

Attention to seldom-seen details adds to the overall beauty of Pointless, and the irony of the chosen title is painful. Nearly every team member was christened by one of the sharply pointed spears jutting from the bike at every junction. Although equipped with a rear swing arm and suspension, the pain offered by Pointless far outweighs the cruel nature of a rigid chassis.

As a self-contained producer, Tempest began construction with a Razorback frame of its own design and assembly. The first of the 25 pointed daggers thrusts forward from the frame's lower down tubes, beginning the theme with a vengeance. This motif is seen again at the

chrome tips on the upward swing of the rear swing arm. By including the chrome spikes on every spear, the point is driven home. With every inch of frame created from ground zero, only the 45-degree rake can be considered part of the geometry. Most other frames are stretched, goosed or raised from their stock dimension, but the Razorback is an original design, carrying its own credentials. A pair of Harley-Davidson fork legs, acquired from a Deuce model, is held in check by Accutronix triple trees. Attached to the top plate of the upper triple tree is a phalanx of pointed steel that would give an insurance adjuster heartburn for a week, but they look great on this scoot.

The 88-cubic-inch Harley motor exhales through a twisted maze of tubes finished in black, chrome and heat tape.

The handlebars' inward contours are another bit of genius from Tempest Cycles, as are the grips, clutch and brake levers, and risers. The foot-controls region holds a vast assortment of swooping, pointed steel, all dipped in chrome for your viewing pleasure. Few outside influences were used in the assembly of this one-off machine. Along with the custom-crafted frame, the Tempest crew hand rolled every section of sheet metal except for the oil tank. The fuel tank's swells and contours accentuate the chassis as it flows into several of the related tubes in the frame's assembly. With 25 lethal points in Pointless' quiver, only a polished metal pillion seemed the right choice.

Tempest once again rolled the saddle from a flat section of alloy, resulting in the unforgiving curves of honed aluminum. Even though the oil bag was taken from a Harley-Davidson Twin Cam, it, too, was modified by integrating the bike's electronics into the component. As if creating the rest of the sheet metal by hand doesn't drive the point home, Tempest took the time and effort to condense and sterilize the remaining requirements of this build-off entry.

Among the few outside parts, Performance Machine Trinity rims are mounted at both axles, and Avon Viper rubber hugs the alloy hoops. A reclusive front master cylinder sends the needed fluid to the Performance

Between the dual-ended and dangerously pointed frame tubes and the weapons-grade foot controls, it's a wonder the rider doesn't need a special permit to mount Pointless.

Nestled among the frame's painfully pointed sections is the air suspension, delivering comfort to the rider.

Any form of upholstery was turned down. Considering the dangerous nature of the rest of the chopper, the polished alloy saddle seems the perfect choice.

With cleanliness in mind, the rear drive combines the pulley and brake rotor into a single unit, thus removing one of the typical distractions from the equation.

Machine brake on the leading wheel, which arrests the Trinity rotor's forward motion. A similar arrangement is used on the rear wheel, completing the slow-down part of the tour.

Under the "go-fast" heading, we find a stock 88-cubic-inch motor from Harley-Davidson fitted with a custom Tempest exhaust. The blacked-out motor is closed off with an array of polished case covers. The exhaust is a virtual snake pit of coiling tubes finished in matte black, trimmed with chrome accents, and wrapped with heat tape.

All in all, Pointless is a well-designed and even better built chopper than many we have seen. The simple theme was executed at a high level despite the painful potential its steel barbs hold for the unaware.

CLASS OF '70

Jim Weller

At this point in chopper history, we are accustomed to the exotic, high-dollar builds we see on television and in print. It seems no expense is spared as builders try to out-do each other with extravagant paint, bizarre frames and huge horsepower. That may be the state of the art, but there was a time when choppers were much simpler. Many early examples were home built,

using whatever hardware was lying around or could be picked up at local swap meets. Although not as flashy or visually stimulating, these early offerings still interest a certain faction of builders and riders.

Jim Weller wanted something that celebrated those simpler days of custom choppers and marked the year of his high-school graduation. Class of '70 was built in the old-world style that is often forgotten today. To accomplish his old-school dreams, Jim wanted nothing to do with contemporary hardware, even if it looked the part. Construction was based on a 1970 Triumph Bonneville frame that was powder coated for

a clean and durable finish. Removing the original sprung swing arm and replacing it with a rigid section of unknown origin added another taste of the early days. Another mystery piece is the old springer front fork, which was powder coated with a near-chrome finish. Before coating, however, the fork needed to be straightened.

The fuel tank is a stock Triumph piece, as is the ribbed rear fender. A Moon Equipment oil bag holds 4 quarts of the slippery stuff and makes a perfect addition to the old-world charm. Modern cylinder mounts came from Fabricator Kevin. Rolling stock is a hodgepodge of Honda, Harley

Power, such as it is, comes from a 1970 500-cc Triumph mill. No nitrous or high-tech trickery here.

and Triumph bits, all joined as one. The 19-inch front spoke wheel is factory Honda; the rear hoop is a Harley rim with a Triumph hub. The 16-inch rear wheel was a common choice back in the day and is in keeping with the build's nature. Even the selected rubber comes from different makers. The front loop is a Super Eagle from Goodyear; the rear is a Michelin Commander. The rear whitewall goes back to the simpler days of chopper building without passing go. Braking is rudimentary in the spool hub and factory drum mounted to the rear rim.

No additional braking power is found on the front wheel, adding to the excitement when a sudden stop is required. Perhaps lucky for Jim, the 500-cc Triumph motor is not capable of frightening amounts of power. Although not the powerhouse we have come to know, it was still rebuilt to assure confidence on the open road. Even a factory-style Amal 626 carburetor was chosen to dole out the fuel to the vertical motor. The blackened exhaust tubes were taken from a Triumph T100C, which places the exit pipe fairly high on the chassis. Taking a cue from the past and a chance at maybe getting a spark, true-to-life Lucas (The Prince of Darkness) points and coil light the bike into action, assuming it's a good day. A

The sprung front fork was coated in near chrome for a look that isn't as dazzling as today's chrome, but isn't meant to be.

A simple and small drum unit on the rear wheel is totally responsible for braking.

The blacked-out exhaust tubes were taken from a Triumph T100C, originally an on- and off-road machine.

simple four-speed gearbox, again from Triumph, limits Jim's ratio options, but he expects nothing more from his two-wheeled time machine.

A handmade loop of steel makes up the sissy bar arched over the rear fender. Additional bits of Jim's know-how are found in the stainless-steel oil lines and control linkage. The tiny sprung saddle is a modern LePera model styled in the shadow of the vintage Bates seat. Only simple black vinyl covers the seat pan, sparing some exotic creature its hide. The chrome coil springs are about the only comfort offered to anyone throwing a leg over the bike, but they should expect nothing more.

Anything that needed paint was coated with a rattle-can finish, otherwise known as spray paint. The early days of choppers didn't know the expanse of high-tech coatings we enjoy today, but maybe were better for it. Instead of simply dropping off our sheet metal at the painter and waiting for the final product, we went into the backyard or basement and did it ourselves. The results weren't as exciting, but the personal factor was a lot higher.

Much of the related hardware on Class of '70 hails from unknown sources. Neither the handlebars, grips, brake and clutch levers, nor taillight have any recorded parental lineage, but we're certain that someone reading this book will be able to point out the exact origin of each piece in question. The classic Iron Cross mirrors are a touch of modern equipment from Goblin Millworx, the same folks responsible for the coating on the front forks.

Working "on and off" for about 18 months, Jim Weller created a bike that suits his contemporary needs while addressing motorcycling's past. For this effort, we send Jim to the head of the class.

TAINTED ANGEL

Thee Darkside Choppers

T hee Darkside Choppers of Daytona Beach, Fla., builds some of the wildest choppers on the East Coast, or any coast for that matter. Pain Eriksson is the man in charge of every facet of the design, creation and assembly. Even the glassy and intricate paint application falls into his capable hands. Never satisfied with what he sees in other machines, including his own, Pain raises the bar with every new model that rolls out of his shop. He doesn't really build them to sell, but usually ends up doing so whenever his mounts hit the streets of Daytona

or other locales he decides to prowl. As hand-built machines go, they don't sell cheaply, but who'd want that anyway? This particular example carries an approximate sticker price just north of $50,000, but considering all the hand-built components, that's a steal.

Pain often bristles when the unwashed ask if his creation is from a certain East Coast builder, but at least people notice his efforts. In a world with more than its share of bike builders, it takes a lot to get noticed these days. And noticed he gets. As a longtime resident of Daytona Beach, which has its share of biker-related activities, Pain's reputation precedes him. The locals know him from 40

Graphics on the fuel tank show the Angel's portrait in subtle yet highly detailed art.

paces, and regular visitors are getting better at it, too. It's hard to miss a guy who stands 6 feet, 4 inches, is covered with tattoos, and sports a kind-of Mohawk hairdo complete with a braided pony tail. He didn't earn his nickname by accident, although he's had his share of those, too.

With every custom he builds, Pain begins with a frame of his own concept. He then crams a mad motor into the tubes. In this instance, a 145-cubic-inch lump from Ultima is the power plant. Never one to leave well enough alone, Pain disassembled the mill to install new hardware that better suits his maniacal needs, or at least his wants. No one needs a massaged 145-cubic-inch motor in their motorcycle, yet the

brutes seem to find their way into Pain's choppers regularly. At least this one isn't supercharged. Custom-produced connecting rods, forged in titanium, hold the 4 1/2-inch-diameter pistons in line.

Many of the motor's internals hail from Crane, and most were modified. The exhaust was, of course, hand bent by Thee Darkside and then chrome plated for long life and great looks. An S&S Super G carburetor handles the intake of fuel and air, and sparks fly from a prototype Crane ignition. Inhaled oxygen is kept clean by a tapered, oval filter from K&N. Gear selection is accomplished with a Delkron case filled with Andrews gears. Three inches of belt transfer the power from motor to gearbox, and a chain handles the final drive.

The 145 cubic inches of brute horsepower are barely contained in the Ultima motor's cases.

The oil tank, with chrome faucet handles, is another hand-formed component.

A rear fender was created by bending half-inch steel rod into this weblike form.

As expected, frame geometry is extreme: 55-degree rake, 12 inches up, 7 inches out. No self-respecting chopper builder would even think of having a rear suspension, so the chassis is rigid. The front fork consists of Midwest legs and Forking by Frank tubes. The entire assembly measures 24 inches over for that long, lean look, and a wide stance adds to the configuration's stability. The extra stretch looks right at home when the tall Pain is in the drop saddle, which is covered in black ostrich hide. Topping off the frame tubes is a variety of chrome spikes, providing no service except to look intimidating. Mission accomplished.

The front hoop is a Jesse James part, and a single disc brake from Performance Machine provides the required anchorage. The rear unit is a Eurocomponents sprotor, which combines the brake rotor and sprocket

into one item. A solid rear wheel from RevTech is polished to mirror-like perfection, and Metzeler rubber (21-inch front, 300-series rear) keeps both rims off the pavement.

Saving the most outlandish detail for last, Pain himself cut, bent, shaped, and welded every inch of sheet metal into its final form. Mimicking a shapely and perfectly symmetrical orange slice, the fuel tank features two pass-through openings and, of course, the requisite spiked fuel cap. Topping off the front-mounted oil bag's compound curves is a pair of chrome faucet handles for easy insertion of the required lubricants. Paint

Pain Eriksson

details expose women wearing little more than a smile and maybe some body ink. Lightly shadowed tribal flames lick the oil tank and under-seat battery compartment. The result is subtle yet effective. The rear fender is a spider's web of half-inch steel rods, commandeered into shape and finished off with a decorative (we hope) grenade.

Headwinds delivers the candlepower for night riding up front, and the ubiquitous Maltese-cross taillight lets people out back know when you're slowing a bit. Handlebars, risers and grips are all components crafted by Thee Darkside, making sure that even common items remain exclusive. An additional set of scantily clad females is used for the front foot pegs and again are products of Pain's warped mind. Don't even ask him where the mirrors or turn signals are; he doesn't believe a bike is righteous if it includes those domesticated items.

These machinations produced a chopper almost 11 feet long, making it look like something from another dimension or at least another planet. It's hard to imagine what Pain Eriksson's next effort will be. Hide the kids.

THANATOS 666

Wes Sturgill and Pain Eriksson

Born from a discussion about frame design, Thanatos 666 is the result of many man-hours, plenty of creativity and more than likely a few cocktails. There are some people who can take the worst of times and still find a ray of sunshine. This build includes several sections of scrap steel that became available after a storm. Well, it was

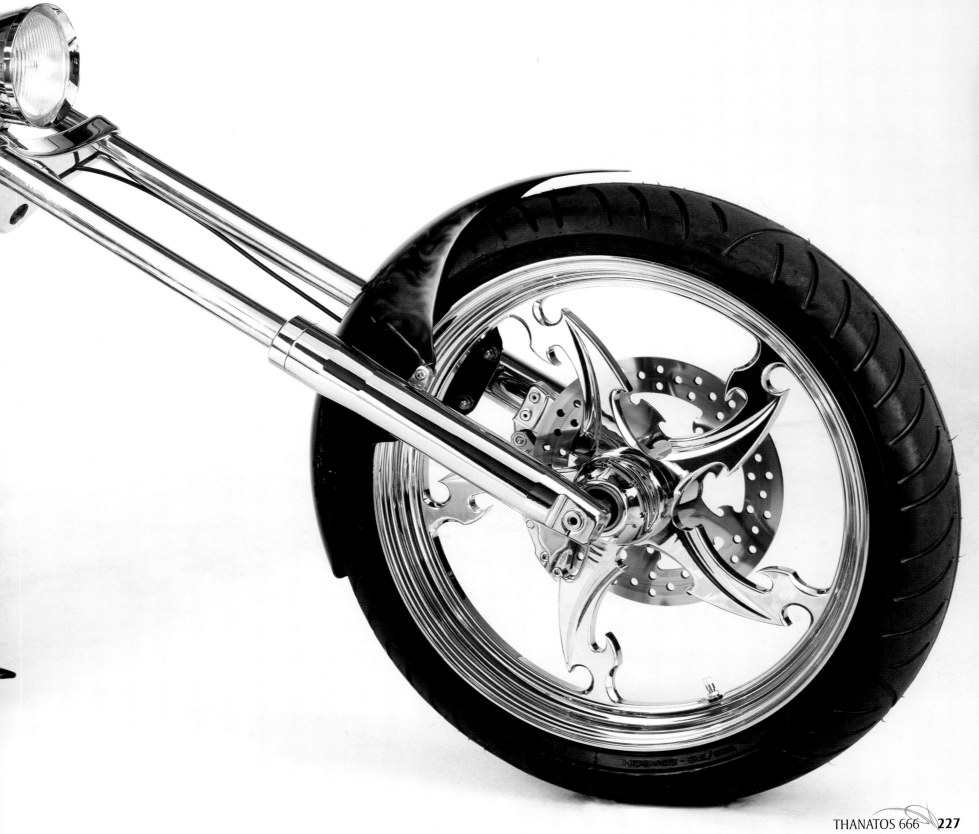

more like a hurricane named Charley, which ripped through Florida in August 2004 causing millions of dollars in damage. Instead of discarding the errant sheet metal, the builders used it for Thanatos 666.

A collaborative effort between the owner and Thee Darkside Choppers of Daytona Beach, Fla., Thanatos 666 may symbolize death, but it gave new life to some old materials. Of course, not all the hardware was tossed aside by the storm. The current market for chopper parts is to blame for filling in the blanks.

With an extreme rake of 70 degrees at the steering head, the Killer Chopper special frame started off the build with a bang. To this rake was added 6 inches over, 8 inches out and a stretch of 10 inches. Long, lean and radical are the result. The Perse Long Neck forks were enhanced by 10 inches and also bring an additional 5 degrees of rake. Actually, the added dose of rake comes from the H&H Machine Clear Tree triple trees.

All of the body panels were formed from random sections of storm-induced metal or, in the fuel tank's case, a retired rear fender. First used

A 127-cubic-inch El Bruto motor from Ultima makes a fitting choice for this exotic build.

Beginning its life as a rear fender, the fuel tank saw extensive modification to become the svelte unit we see here.

to cover a 280-series rear tire, the fender's metal was reworked and now carries the precious cargo in its shapely contours. The oil storage tank was formed from a section of water pipe, thus proving that even custom-chopper builders are into recycling. The seat pan, which was formed by wrapping it around a palm tree, and front and rear fenders were all created from metal segments strewn by Charley. It was no easy task to create such beautiful shapes from scrap, but Darkside Choppers has years of practice doing just that. The rear fender also hides the electronics and required switches,

and a remote battery resides beneath the transmission.

It takes more than scrap metal to make a high-end custom chopper, so the build team turned to a variety of sources to complete the project. A 4-inch by 21-inch Slayer rim from Wicked Image carries Avon Venom-X rubber at the forks, and the rigid frame holds a 12-inch by 18-inch solid disc hoop from Rev-Tech. An expansive 300-series tire, also an Avon Venom-X, leaves its footprint on the Florida streets for all to see. Exile Cycles was tapped for the front and rear brake rotors, as well as the rear

![A modified S&S Super G carb was paired with a Darkside Choppers air cleaner.]()

A modified S&S Super G carb was paired with a Darkside Choppers air cleaner.

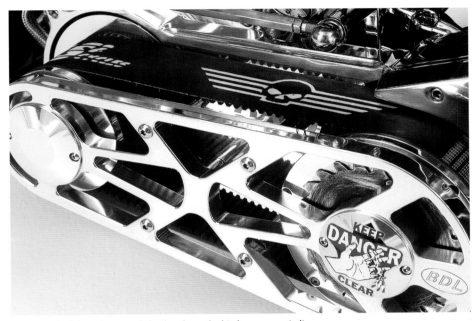

BDL supplied the primary and clutch to keep the big horsepower in line.

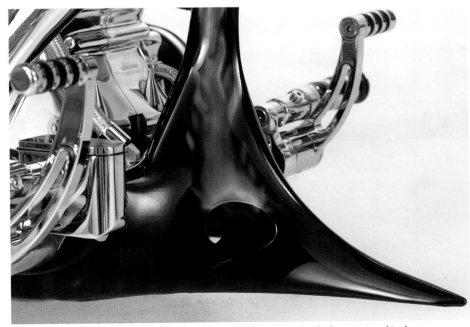

The frame's front down tube was augmented by an evil-looking beak, which was painted in the same motif as the rest of the bodywork.

A Wicked Image Slayer front wheel leads the assembly down the road with its chromed surfaces gleaming.

caliper. Performance Machine supplied the leading caliper, and the mix does an adequate job of bringing Thanatos 666 to a halt.

Keeping the bike between the curbs is a set of handlebars and risers from H&H Machine. The low-mounted, drag-style bars make handling more precise, especially when you're steering a 75-degree rake. Arlen Ness grips and a mirror by the owner finish off the list of upper controls. BDL delivered the foot pegs and controls, although Wes altered

them. A cool set of retractable rear foot pegs slides into the frame when not being used and snaps into a locked position when duty calls. This aspect of the build also was handmade but obviously is subtle.

Motoring Thanatos 666 along is an El Bruto V-twin from Ultima. The 127 cubic inches of displacement are

teamed with an enviable list of racing-quality bits and pieces. Wiseco pistons are mounted to Carillo connecting rods, and titanium valves are bumped into action by Crane 700 cams. A modified S&S Super G carburetor is topped off with an original Darkside Choppers air cleaner, and a custom-fabricated exhaust from OTTI Cycles wraps up the motivation division. Taking the extra steps to ensure a clean appearance, the builders ran the spark-plug wires through the cylinder heads,

keeping them out of sight. A Baker six-speed tranny is matched with a BDL clutch and primary, which send the chosen ratios to the rear wheel with a Tsubaki chain. An Exile sprocket-rotor combo translates the power to the rear donut.

According to the owner and builder, it took almost a year to complete Thanatos 666, including a few breaks for some liquid inspiration.

LAST MINUTE

Stephenson Motorsports

Stephenson Motorsports can provide the at-home builder with a catalog of limited-production components, or it can build a complete machine to suit his tastes and pocketbook. The talented staff melds many abilities with few limitations.

Last Minute is another chopper built to compete in the 2005 Heritage Motorcycle Rally Bike Build-Off in Charleston, S.C. One of only 10 builders invited to the event, Stephenson Motorsports put this example together in six months.

With its own line of sheet metal and frames, Stephenson didn't have to turn to outside vendors for much of this creation. The basis for the build is a Nightmare frame of Stephenson's design. Complete with an integrated oiling system, the chassis rides on a rake of 52 degrees with 2 inches over, 7 inches out and 2 inches under the stock numbers. Holding the front rim in line is a Wide Glide fork from HHI that was extended 2 inches. HHI 41-millimeter triple trees hold the sleek tubes together. A 21-inch Viper rim from Carolina Custom Products is bound by a Metzeler tire. Front braking comes from a Carolina Custom Products Viper rotor as well. A six-piston unit from Performance Machine places pressure on the disc. Although the chassis' rear end lacks suspension, it does carry another Viper wheel and is fitted with a matching rotor. A four-piston model from Performance Machine stops the motion, and front and rear brakes are activated by a solitary foot pedal. This linked system frees up the handlebar of one control lever and adds a measure of safety for the rider.

A curved and toothed dagger was selected for Last Minute's shift lever, replacing a more typical device.

A brightly polished Total Performance motor displaces 113 cubic inches and features a Crane 600 cam to control the valves. A Crane HI-4 ignition provides the spark, and an S&S Model G carburetor metes out the fuel as needed. Stephenson Motorsports is responsible for the two-into-two exhaust that snakes toward the scooter's rear. Unlike many choppers today, Last Minute shifts through a five-speed gearbox instead of a six. The Baker unit is bolted to a Karata primary, adapted for use by Stephenson Motorsports, and a Barnett clutch provides the needed slippage for the drive chain.

Stephenson is to blame for the sensuous sheet metal, including the Radius fuel tank. This model swells and swoops its way back to the Old Stage saddle, covered in alligator pelt. Although hidden from view, the oil bag is another SMS item and deserves to be exposed.

The tight-radius front fender reaches around about 50 percent of the front tire and matches the diameter like a second skin. The rear fender also does a more than adequate job of concealing the giant 280-series donut but allows enough to be viewed for our pleasure. The handlebars, which lack second-

Although rigid, the chassis' rear section looks like a fluid section of steel.

Mounted in the "V" of the SMS bars is a monitor that shows the rider who he has just passed.

The SMS-crafted chin spoiler cleans up the air flow and looks terrific at the same time.

ary risers, carry a set of Accutronix grips to accent the color-matched SMS tubes. The bars are devoid of the usual rear-view mirrors but do house a small monitor coupled to a small camera, which delivers a detailed view of where you've just been. The SMS foot pegs and forward controls flank a smoothly contoured chin spoiler that carries the intricate paint scheme one step further. House of Kolor hues – including aqua, silver, blue, orange, and yellow – were integrated into the tribal graphics theme.

Amazingly, Jerry's Last Minute did not place in the top three in the build-off. For a machine that carries this much handcrafted ingenuity and specialty hardware not to win, you can imagine how stiff the competition was.

PANHANDLER

Skunkworx Custom Cycles

Some may equate the term "skunk works" with the undercover government operation that built the SR-71 Blackbird. Others may recall the early days of the Andy Capp cartoon, which also featured a skunk-works reference.

No matter what comes to mind for you, Bruce Mullins assembles a diverse collection of custom cycles under his "Skunkworx" version. Based in Columbus, Ohio, the shop is easy to find, unlike the secretive military effort of the same name. Skunkworx welcomes

visitors to purchase parts, view the current builds, or tell Bruce what he can put together for them.

Panhandler is another custom mount built to compete in the 2005 Heritage Motorcycle Rally Bike Build-Off in Charleston, S.C. Skunkworx was one of only 10 builders selected to compete. Bruce intended to build a contest bike that joined old- and new-world features into a single unit,

thus appealing to both ends of the spectrum. His innovative features included some vintage touches, and together they did well at the event.

A Skunkworx frame carries the balance of the hardware in a stylish and effective package. The lower down tubes are highlighted by a set of drilled flying buttresses that also add some rigidity to the mix. A fairly mild 47-degree rake was accented by another 4 inches out to make sure

The split fuel tank carries oil in one half and gas in the other. It looks fully finished from any angle.

Panhandler was as rideable as it was attractive. The heavily tubed Dragon springer front fork hails from American Suspension. The lower segments are powder coated in black. Two inches added to the fork give the riding stance Bruce desired.

Complementing the sprung front fork's old-world styling is a 106-cubic-inch Panhead motor from Accurate Engineering. Built with nothing but the best in contemporary hardware, it carries the bits and pieces in a housing designed to look like it was borrowed from a 1940s Harley-Davidson. The Super G carburetor from S&S provides modern fuel consumption and is topped off with a Skunkworx air cleaner. The Mallory Unilite ignition delivers the spark. Exiting gases travel through a Tubular Techniques exhaust modified by Skunkworx before installation.

The brushed stainless finish adds to the retro-looking chopper's patina. Six speeds from Baker roll through a BDL clutch, primary and final drive. Hard lines route the fuel and oil to the appointed destinations, adding a bit of laboratory cleanliness to that side of the V-twin. Continuing on the vintage trail, we find Ride Wright spoked wheels at each end, with Ego Tripp Spoke brake rotors halted by Performance Machine calipers.

The Ego Tripp Spoke rotor mimics wheels of the same name and provides a durable home for the drive chain's abuse.

The BDL primary is shown with the hard-line fuel and oil routing, which adds a new level of clean to the build.

Decorative and structural, these flying buttresses do double duty on Panhandler.

Skunkworx went way outside the box in creating Panhandler's body-work. The fuel tank consists of two individual sections hinged at the steering head, allowing them to be swung open. The left half of the tank actually stores the motor oil When opening the tank, you find some detailed paint work on the inside panels, showing that Bruce left no stone unturned in building this show bike.

The rear fender is mounted to the chassis' central spine, eliminating the need for the sometimes awkward struts that support the rear form. Many of these features go unnoticed at first glance but become more apparent as the viewer absorbs the assembly's details. Skunkworx modified the Headwinds headlight to hold the digital speedometer in the nacelle's rear taper.

The brake lamp came from a 1939 Ford and also was altered for use. Skunkworx handlebars and grips are finished off with control levers from Performance Machine. The foot pegs and controls are all Skunkworx. The hand-tooled leather saddle is another Skunkworx product. Its rough-hewn design brings yet another touch of a bygone era. The battery, electrics and wiring are tucked away from view, adding to the build's clean, surgical precision.

It required five months to assemble, but Panhandler was completed alongside other bikes being built by Skunkworx for other shows and customers. I highly doubt that a covert government crew could achieve the same.

COBRA 2

Fearless Choppers

When building Cobra 2, Martin Dring combined two schools of thought into a single, artful unit. His Fearless Choppers is known for turning out some radical yet rider-friendly bikes, and this example follows in those tire tracks. Martin takes great care to build choppers that are not only beautiful but can be ridden easily and safely.

One stigma he hoped to avoid was the "bolt-on" look of many other cycles. To eliminate that faux pas, Fearless Choppers welded the primary segments of sheet metal into place, creating a seamless, one-piece assembly. The fuel tank flows smoothly into the frame, which is met by

the sculpted rear fender, also melded into the chassis. Martin also wanted to avoid the trend to hide from view anything mechanical. He believes choppers are "mechanical pieces of art" and therefore should be proud to show off what makes them run. Although his concepts contrast one another, the result is spectacular.

The Cobra 2 fuel tank was formed by Fearless Choppers and then welded onto the Precious Metal Customs Spoon chassis. The tank engulfs the upper frame tube and appears to swallow the steering head as well. Only a triangular opening in the sheet metal hints that we aren't viewing

a solid slab of steel. This choice runs with fairly steep geometry but remains stable when ridden. Six inches over and 5 inches out were added to the 52-degree rake, throwing the front end way out in front of the rider. Mean Street forks and triple trees were implemented for precise steering, even though the fork legs are 24 inches over the factory specs. The trees hold another 7 degrees of rake, claiming partial responsibility for the bike's long dimension.

Compounding the terrific handling is the set of Fearless Customs 73-millimeter, clamp-on handlebars. Looking like something borrowed from

The L.M.F. exhaust provides resistance to the rushing fumes as they exit the motor.

Xtreme Machine Twisted wheels roll at either end of Cobra 2 – 21 inches up front and 18 out back.

◄ Mid-USA provided the 114-cubic-inch Powerhouse motor installed in the Precious Metal Customs Spoon frame.

a bridge, these massive bars bring steering control to a new level. The rider's hands fall onto a set of Death Spear grips from Thunder Cycle and squeeze levers by Performance Machine. A 21-inch, 120-millimeter Avon Venom tire is wrapped around an Xtreme Machine Twisted rim for accurate control. A matching Twisted brake rotor is hugged by an HHI six-piston caliper to provide smooth stops.

The three-dimensional rear fender also is welded directly to the frame to continue the seamless theme. In addition to the welded mounting, the fender

Martin Dring

is fully molded into the chassis. Beneath the steel rolls a 300-millimeter Avon Venom, again stretched around an Xtreme Machine Twisted hoop. A four-piston HHI caliper slows another matching rotor. No one wants to build a chopper that's all show and no go, and Fearless is no different. A

Mid-USA 114-cubic-inch Powerhouse mill was selected for Cobra 2 and does a fine job of motivating the long bike down the road. A Mikuni 48-millimeter carburetor gets clean air through the Wimmer Super-Sucker filter. The L.M.F. pipe from Creative Cycles leads the spent gases away in a hurry. The two-into-one system was treated to a matte black finish, then highlighted with a chrome "V" and equally polished tip. Baker provides six speeds and uses a Primo clutch for easy selection.

The Galaxy Grey and Silver paint from House of Kolor adds an ethereal quality to the build and is well suited to the sheet metal's shapes and contours. A snakeskin saddle adds the finishing touch to this long, powerful and usable chopper. Who said mechanical can't be beautiful?

NEGATIVE IMAGE

Precious Metal Customs

uss Austin began to bend and wrench his own customs mainly because his budget wouldn't permit him to pay someone else. The more time he spent on his early projects, the more apparent it became that he had a knack for the work. Time marched on, and soon even frames from outside vendors were not satisfactory. To fulfill his lofty standards, Russ created the Spoon rigid chassis. This frame embodies a radical geometry and drastically low saddle height. The single down tube is massive and helps provide the stiffness required for today's powerful customs.

Russ Austin

Of course, assembly for his latest creation began with his own Spoon chassis, but Russ wanted to go in a direction different from other customs. After attending numerous events and viewing other choppers, he soon realized that designs often focused on chrome. To overcome this trend, he chose the mostly black motif for Negative Image. Although a certain amount of chrome was used, some primary components were dipped in black to complete the illusion.

Leading the way is a set of 63-millimeter forks from American Suspension. That is a huge number in today's cycle market; even the raciest of sport bikes carries only 50-millimeter tubes. Eighteen inches were added to the fork legs, putting the front wheel way out in front of the rider. Adding to the tubes' altered appearance is the glossy black coating applied to the forks. The shaved upper tree and lower unit were also dipped in black. Only the fork tubes' sliding sections were left untreated. Frantic

PMC crafted the Scoop tank from flat sheet metal and graced it with a detailed paint job that accentuates the form's curves.

wheels from Xtreme Machine, finished in chrome, are mounted to both axles. The stubby, clip-on-style handlebars are another PMC product and ride beneath the upper triple tree, in contrast with many other bikes. Their 63-millimeter diameter makes a strong statement, in tune with the rest of the bike. Excel Components is responsible for the Wicked grips, brake and clutch levers, foot pegs, and controls.

The Scoop fuel tank, another PMC item, is curvaceous and presents a multitude of shapes for our eyes to absorb. The raised central spine and side panels feature sharp yet softened angles made more exciting by Ghost Chrome paint. A triangular chin spoiler also is grafted with some subtle shaping and equally detailed paint. This spoiler is blended artfully into the down tube and lower frame rails, becoming one with the metal. The absence of front and rear fenders also flies in the face of convention as well as certain regional laws.

The shaved triple tree carries the 63-millimeter handlebars milled by Russ Austin at PMC.

A Medieval chin spoiler, blended into the frame tubes, adds to Negative Image's custom metal.

Martin Bros. exhaust pipes sweep the fumes away in one clean motion and bring a touch of chrome to the predominantly black motor.

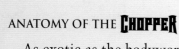

As exotic as the bodywork and concept are, the motor is a standard Harley-Davidson 80-cubic-inch V-twin. The Evo motor, however, is trimmed in all black, including the 42-millimeter Mikuni carb and single velocity stack. Even the BDL primary was finished in black, which cuts heavily into the standard application of chrome. A pair of Martin Bros. exhaust tubes, dipped in lustrous chrome, save the day.

In charge of bringing the fast-moving scooter to a halt are Frantic rotors on both wheels. A six-piston Hawg Halter caliper on the front rim and four-piston unit on the rear provide more than ample power when stopping is a must. The 300-millimeter Venom rubber from Avon places plenty of emphasis on acceleration and leaves a prominent mark when required.

Self taught in the arts of metal shaping, welding and assembly, Russ Austin apparently had a great teacher. Only three weeks were needed to make Negative Image a moving piece of sculpture, adding immensely to Russ' growing legion of fans.

BUILDERS LIST

American Iron Horse
4600 Blue Mound Road
Fort Worth, TX 76106
(817) 665-2000
www.americanironhorse.com

BREW Bikes LLC
1241 Industrial Parkway
West Jefferson, NC 28694
(336) 246-8555
www.brewracingframes.com

Britt Custom Metrix
6789 Market St.
Wilmington, NC 28405
(910) 791-8321
www.brittcustommetrix.com

Carolina Custom Choppers
211 Williamsburg County Highway North
Kingstree, SC 29556
(843) 201-6202
www.russellmarlowe.com

Chopsmiths
100 Gasoline Alley   Suite B
Indianapolis, IN 46222
(317) 246-7737
www.handbuiltmotorcycles.com

Jeff Cooper
513 Howard Court
Fairmount, IN 46928
(765) 948-4263
Slider13@frontier.net

Custom Shop Cycles
206 S. Main
Flanagan, IL 61740
(815) 796-2772
www.customshop.org

Dino's Custom Cycles
7855 W. 16th Ave.
Lakewood, CO 80214
(303) 233-1600
dinoscycles@earthlink.net

Echelon Motorcycles
2320 W. Airport Blvd.
Sanford, FL 32771
(407) 322-0095
www.echelonmotorcycles.com

Exile Cycles
13209 Saticoy St.
North Hollywood, CA 91605
(818) 768-7667
www.exilecycles.com

Fabricator Kevin's Steel Chopper Parts
44306 Macomb Industrial Drive
Clinton Township, MI 48036
(586) 465-2600
www.fabkevin.com

Fearless Choppers
150 Sweetmans Lane
Manalapan, NJ 07726
(732) 221-0825
www.fearlesschoppers.com

Kingpin Custom Cycles
3625 Wow Road
Corpus Christi, TX 78413
(361) 806-0464
www.kingpincustomcycles.com

Warren Lane
P.O. Box 655234
Miami, FL 33265
(305) 389-0608
www.theneighborhoodking.com

Mad Creations Custom Cycles
348 Mason Ave.
Daytona Beach, FL 32117
(386) 253-1738
www.madcreationscustomcycles.com

Mad Wrench Custom Cycles
4911 E. Broadway
Tampa, FL 33605
(813) 248-4443
www.thewrenchonline.com

Precious Metal Customs
488 Hendon Road
Woodstock, GA 30188
(678) 687-9361
www.preciousmetalcustoms.com

Pugliese Custom Cycles
6 Whitwell Place
Staten Island, NY 10304
(917) 731-7517
www.pugliesecustomcycles.com

Redneck Engineering
107 Nix Road
Liberty, SC 29657
(864) 843-3001
www.redneckengineering.com

Road-Hawgs
811 Industrial Blvd.
Crown Point, IN 41807
(219) 661-4894
www.road-hawgs.com

Speedway Choppers
140-B Gasoline Alley
Indianapolis, IN 46222
(317) 243-8994
www.speedwaychoppers.com

Skunkworx Custom Cycles
572 S. Nelson Road
Columbus, OH 43205
(614) 372-0316
www.skunkworxcc.com

Stephenson Motorsports
4159 Maria St.
Oxford, NC 27565
(919) 427-1326
www.stephensonmotorsports.com

Tempest Cycles Inc.
6922 Sonny Dale Drive
Melbourne, FL 32904
(321) 724-0601
www.tempestcycles.com

Thee Darkside Choppers
P.O. Box 11324
Daytona Beach, FL 32120
(386) 527-5877
jadedpain@cfl.rr.com

Voodoo Choppers
313 South St.
Rochester, MI 48307
(248) 601-3000
www.voodoochoppers.com

Wide Open Cycles
157 Carswell Ave.
Daytona Beach, FL 32117
(386) 258-8933
www.wideopencycles.com